Attaboy

James Scurti

Published by James Scurti, 2022.

ATTABOY

First edition. December 15, 2022.

Copyright © 2022 James Scurti.

ISBN: 979-8215317686

Written by James Scurti.

Table of Contents

Attaboy is dedicated to my parents and my loving children. Special thanks to Joan Wood for her inspiration, to my Editor, Barbara Gray, and to Graham Jones for his steady support and guidance.

In my five decades in the business, I have probably met and worked with thousands of professionals like myself, who contributed their skills, efforts and energies to produce quality television for millions of viewers around the world. All of them have their stories, most of which will never be heard. I dedicate this book to them also.

Introduction

I never thought I would write a book. No one who knew me thought that either. Frankly, there was little reason for anyone to assume I would ever accomplish anything worthwhile. Deemed unfit for my family's used car business, with no "killer instinct" or demonstrable head for salesmanship, it was hard to contemplate where my future lay. Ridiculously shy and non-aggressive, I showed no aptitude for athletics or academics. My years at college were unexceptional. The temporary jobs that had provided me with spending money were strictly manual labor or otherwise futureless. I was walking around with a "BEST IF USED BY" date on my body and soul. I was reminded of that bleak personal assessment one afternoon while waiting to rehearse a reunion of sorts with the English rock band, "The Who." Roger Daltrey wandered up to my camera position and began to talk to me, just idle chatter, impromptu musings. After a lull in the conversation he said, "I never dreamed I'd be a singer, a rock and roll singer. I was going to be one of those blokes who works in a factory... you know... clock in clock out... after work pint with the lads... home to the missus. Yet here I am." "Here WE were!" was my unspoken response. His admission surprised me by its intimacy and confessional nature. Two men working together, born worlds and an ocean apart, each marveling at where life and fate had brought them.

Anyone lucky enough to be a part of the more visible aspects of the entertainment industry, understands that it is equal parts glamor, glitz, and groveling. Praying for work or for a few days off, true feast or famine. I have known weeks when uncashed paychecks lay on my dresser because I had been too busy to deposit them and other times when credit cards paid the mortgage. Anyone other than family, who knew that I worked in television, assumed I must be rich. Contractor estimates immediately doubled.

After watching my camera's viewfinder for years, I developed a concentrated stare. It unsettled some people, made me seem too "intense." I no longer observed something like a bird or automobile moving, I would "track" it visually until it vanished. The insecurity of freelancing produced nightmares in which I was sliding down a steep roof, my feet pushing the people behind me into free fall while the legs and shoes of others pushed down on me. Dreams where I had lost my way after lunch and couldn't find the studio where I was supposed to be working. I had seen grown men vomiting from the pressure, while others dulled the anxiety and shakes by getting thoroughly stoned and drunk. Crew people were sometimes fired on the spot. Despite the unions, most freelancers could be let go at any time. You could never be certain that you would be there the following day or fired with an email on the ride home. Most shows lasted only a few days. Camera operators were generally the last crew hired and the first to be released when the show "wrapped" and the talent had bolted to their waiting limos. On one of the shows in which I worked, the crew asked if Production would be getting rooms in anticipation of the blizzard threatening New York City that night as other daytime shows were doing. We were told, "No one gets out early, no one is getting a room, and I don't care how the fuck you get home or back here tomorrow!"

If there was an outdoor location shoot, we sometimes stood in the rain. There were times when the falling snow swirled between my eyes and the viewfinder. On other shoots the heat was so intense that the cameras themselves rebelled with electronic glitches and shutdowns. Case in point, any New Year's Eve show shot live in Times Square. Cold wind numbed the fingers, made eyes tear and produced shivers as you stood in place for hours. Concerts often brought bottles, cans, and errant frisbees tossed by drunken fans, missiles that could easily cause serious damage. Twice I had guns pointed at me and received threats of having my ass beat by jerk offs I had never seen before.

Although we freelance camera people are competitors, we are still able to maintain bonhomie... watch out for each other and provide assistance if we see it is needed. Actual grudges are rare. Often, it's simply a matter of respecting another operator's abilities, a variant on the old military adage, "Hate the wearer but respect the uniform!"

Our extended freelance family is a praiseworthy collection of skilled operators indifferent to gender, race, nationality, or age restrictions. When your phone stops ringing and email offers of work stops, you're retired. No handshakes, gold watches, or parties, maybe a few drinks together. Any of us is only as good as our current skill set or "last zoom." It is an amazing business and has been a marvelously interesting and rewarding career for me.

It's time now to pack the dark clothing into my suitcase, print my boarding pass and head to the airport, eventually to meet up with a laughing and loitering group of similarly clad crew in their "show blacks" which in theory, make us invisible to the audience. These days when work, all I need to know is what time dinner is scheduled, where my camera is and what time the show expects to "wrap!" I hope you will enjoy the stories I have chosen to share. Thanks for reading them.

Sincerely,

Jim Scurti

HOW IT STARTED

I guess you could honestly say that my career path began with my playing hooky. The oldest of three brothers, I was the only one of the sons that the local cops did not know by reputation, by name or by sight. Being a truant was not something that anyone who knew me would expect of me, including me! I was "the good kid," never in trouble. My mom's friends all liked me. Their husbands would concur, saying, "That's Joe and Phyllis' oldest boy, he's a "Good Kid."

The mantle of Good Kid fit me all too well, so I decided to stretch its behavioral fabric by skipping school for a day. It would be easy enough for me to do. I routinely left for my bus before anyone else in the family was even up.

So that eventful morning, I stayed in my bedroom, sitting quietly, door closed. Soon enough there came the sounds of my family getting ready for their day. My brothers left for the bus. How would my hooky day go, I wondered? We lived in a rural area of New Jersey. Without a car or license, my options were limited. There wouldn't be much to do but watch television and amuse myself with hours of daytime programming, a parade of game shows and soap operas. I was already missing the companionship of my brothers. Perhaps some advance planning would have been smart.

My parents were talking quietly in the kitchen. Their parental duties done successfully, the boys off to school with no lunches or books forgotten. Soon they too would leave. My dad would drive to work, and my mom would head to the hospital where she was a volunteer. The minutes ticked by. Suddenly, the kitchen phone rang. Not a good sign. It was too early in the day for a casual call. My father answered it, then fell silent. He was listening intently. There had been

1

no jovial greeting. I heard him say, "No, he's not here... he left for school already." There was more silent listening. No, this was not good.

He then said, "OK, I'll check and see if he's here." The very idea that I would be anywhere but in school was preposterous. Nevertheless, my dad yelled up to the second floor where our bedrooms were. "Jimmie, are you upstairs... are you still here?"

Snagged. "Yeah dad," was my embarrassed response. Totally caught... a goddamn, rookie failure. "Thank you nurse for calling... we appreciate your concern." The phone was re-cradled with a worrisome force.

The shit was about to hit that ever-struggling fan. I was the Good Boy, the one my dad never had to leave work for and the son my mom never had to meet with in the principal's office. My delinquency was very bad news for my parents, a sundering in their trust, a shifting of the sands beneath our stable home.

The kindly nurse had merely been worried when I was a no show at school. She was concerned about my health because I was one of the very few "Good Kids." Her appraisal of my character was based strictly on my behavior and not on my academic performance. Even the teachers who really liked me had no problem throwing D's and F's my way as though they were gifts of candy.

At high school graduation, I placed among the bottom five students. Two of the kids were immigrants who never quite picked up the language, there was one guy no one had ever seen and another who never spoke with anyone, didn't eat lunch, and wore his street clothes in gym class. Many years earlier, in grammar school, a nun asked me in front of the entire class if I was supposed to be in that grade. Not her specific class mind you, she thought I had somehow been advanced a year beyond my cognitive abilities. Lesson learned that day, abject humiliation.

It had not helped my case in high school when I received a minus 10 on a Spanish language test. My actual score was zero, but the "generous" Nun deducted 10 points because I misspelled the Spanish word for April, leaving me with a score of less than zero! I had even cheated off the guy who sat next to me, Jose. He got a 25. When I asked him how it was possible for someone named Jose to fail a Spanish Language test, he said that he didn't speak Spanish, he spoke Puerto Rican.

Back to the trouble at hand. My father and mother were the poster children of parental anxiety and concern. Their main question was simply "Why?" There was some definite "WHAT THE FUCK WERE YOU THINKING?" energy lurking within their expressions. "Why did I skip school?" My immediate unspoken answer was an incredibly obvious, "Why Not?" School sucked, it was boring, assholes picked on me, and I had no friends; not one. The real question should have been "Why did you wait so long to do it?"

Two confused parents and their no longer quite so good eldest son sat at the kitchen table. The wall clock ticked loudly in the awkward silence. I fully expected to be immediately driven back to school. Fate had other plans for me, however. My dad decided to take me into New York City for the afternoon.

This was certainly not meant as a reward of any kind. It was more like a desperate "Hail Mary Pass" thrown by an anxious father in the hope of discovering what his usually best-behaved kid's true intentions were. Just how far from the Path of Righteousness had I strayed?

Was my truancy a one-off act of rebellion or the opening shot of a trend? When my younger brothers learned about it later, they were highly amused that their "Can do no wrong" older brother finally did something worthwhile, even if I was caught immediately. Maybe there was hope for me yet!

My dad and I took the train to Penn Station and had lunch at a restaurant under its enormous soon to be criminally demolished roof. Worried father and contrite son were soon walking uptown on Sixth Avenue. It was a great day for a ramble, something neither of us usually did. Frankly, Scurti men never walked or ran unless it was from something, such as imminent arrest, a raging fire, or the unexpected appearance of deep, fast rushing water where there shouldn't be any. Simply to run for the sake of running was a laughable waste of energy. We were strictly fight or flight types. Athletic socks on my feet are simply "white" socks.

Somewhere around 49th street, an ABC Production Assistant offered us tickets to attend the taping of the game show, "THE PRICE IS RIGHT." It was something that neither of we two film and TV fanatics had ever done before and one of those remarkable things that makes New York City so magical.

We grabbed at the offer and were escorted into an intimidating skyscraper and up to the studio where the show would be shot.

"THE PRICE IS RIGHT" was one of my Italian grandmother's favorite daytime shows. Many times, I watched it with her. I was the only one of we kids that she would allow to stay at her home because, need I remind you who the best behaved kid was? Where my brothers were exiled to remained a mystery.

We would sit together in the living room and let the cool blue light flash over us while the amiable host, Bill Cullen, attempted to send prize hungry contestants home with state of the art appliances and trips to any hotel willing to donate all-inclusive stays at their resort, for promotional consideration, of course. Guess who ended up paying the tax on the full, non-discounted suggested retail price of this luxury freebie? That's when the real contestant screaming began!

My grandmother was a very judgmental, opinionated, and thoroughly partisan viewer. She had complete contempt for any player who was not Italian and fervently hoped that the non-Italian Americans lost quickly, to make room for the Italian American contestants whose places they had usurped. This criticism was freely vocalized, usually vulgar, and often racist. No pejorative insult was too strong. No negative assessment of intellect or lineage was too hurtful or undeserved. The harried players were "stupid things" and "foreign morons!" More than once I turned my young head to look at her and ask myself, "Holy shit... do other grandmothers behave this way?"

Meanwhile, jumping ahead to 1964, my dad and I were seated in audience rows arranged in tiers. The people around us seemed to have been recruited, just like us, from the apparent army of souls wandering aimlessly around Midtown Manhattan on any given day, just waiting for what the city would offer them next, like tickets to a famous game show!

The audience members spoke in hushed, respectful conversations. We were all slightly intimidated by the frenzied activity on display in front of us. Great groups of large, intensely bright lights were suspended from the crisscross grid of metal pipes above us. I'm sure we were not the only ones wondering what their electric bill must be monthly. On the wood stage, men and a scattering of women scurried across the gleaming floor. Large cameras were rolled into place. Microphones hanging from booms attached to other platforms were wheeled into position. Every activity was carried out quickly and orderly. There was a near mechanical process of this going here and that there. When the models began to walk out onto the stage, the audience reacted with excited murmurs of approval and excitement. This was really going to happen, and soon.

The women were dressed in fashionable skirts and outfits. They laughed together with teasing nonchalance, as though appearing on a nationally televised program watched by millions, was a very simple and matter of fact activity. For these beautiful women, it probably was. How many of the females in the assembled audience around me imagined themselves in one of those gorgeous gowns, fussed over by makeup and hair people whose sole job was to turn attractive into beautiful, remarkable into gorgeous, to make the casually observed, unforgettable.

I had a favorite among the models as a result of years of viewing. Her name was June. She was the only one whose name I remembered. My grandmother complimented her often, high praise indeed. June had the most sincere smile and the warmest, most generous personality. She radiated control, charm, and class. She blessed each of the prizes with special importance. Every 12-cup percolator, kitchen range, and especially those shiny automobiles which drew gasps from the audience, were graced with need to have value simply by reason of her gesturing to it as if to say, "Here is not just a toaster but the FIRST among toasters... the World's ULTIMATE toaster. And it could be YOURS for the winning today on "THE PRICE IS RIGHT!" Always done with a cheerful, charming smile, even I could tell that she was more than a model; she was probably a great human being. She was a real gal.

We laughed at the warmup guy's jokes, promised to obey the show's rules, and applauded with genuine excitement whenever the "APPLAUSE" sign flashed into life. We shared vicariously in the contestant's excitement, felt their stress, exulted in their successes. The 60 or so minutes raced by. Once Cullen and the models had waved goodnight and left the stage, we were escorted back onto Manhattan's teeming streets to resume our regular existence and ordinary lives. I have to admit though, that we did feel special having had the experience. After all, it's not every day you get to walk onto the stage of a television production. Little did I know the personal significance of this serendipitous event. None of the disinterested and preoccupied pedestrians was even aware of how special we were, or how extraordinary our afternoon had been. After dinner at Tad's Steakhouse, a family favorite, we took the train back to Trenton. There was no further mention of my stunt nor any expectation it would ever be repeated.

Eventually I crawled out of high school and into a string of colleges where my academic record improved slightly. I had interests, girlfriends, and even buddies but still no real direction in life. When an opportunity to work at a television station presented itself, I took it, receiving my college degrees at a later date.

Two decades later, that same model June was my Mother-In-Law, I was an Emmy Award winning cameraman, and working on that same stage doing one of the several shows I did for the network. Sometimes I would glance up from the stage floor, look at the audience, and remember that afternoon with my dad.

Like much in my life, I had simply wandered into something great. On that day with him, I had not left the game show studio determined to seek a career in TV production. It was beyond even my vivid imagination. Sure, it was a dazzling experience, but the rest of high school and four years of college loomed ahead of me.

My future, at that teen age was opaque, but had you asked me, it certainly would not have included anything like a career, let alone in a glamorous profession. We had no contact with anyone in entertainment, no one to pull strings or crack open any doors.

It did seem in retrospect as though Fate had been teasing me, giving me a peek into my own future, with stunning accuracy. Maybe having a laugh at my expense; no matter.

If you imagine for a moment that Life is a gameshow, then I emerged a winner. I had collected prizes more durable and valuable than toasters, trips, and even cars. I had married into a wonderful, loving family and been blessed with two extraordinary children. I had enjoyed a long and marvelous career, gifted with exotic travel, lasting friendships, and incredible experiences. What if I had trudged off to school as expected that long ago morning, would my life have changed? Personally, I believe I owe it all to playing hooky.

Now please allow me to commence with these stories from my life and "Get the show on the road!" Enjoy.

BRIEF ENCOUNTERS WITH CAMELOT

1976

It was my first year at the ABC Network. I was stressed out and overtired from double shifts on the hit soap opera "RYAN'S HOPE" in the morning and Network National news or NYC local news during the afternoon and into the night. "RYAN'S HOPE" was set in New York City. Its convoluted story line followed the lives, troubles, and dreams of an Irish-American family whose parents ran a bar in "Hell's Kitchen," New York's traditional Irish ghetto. The family's eldest son was an up-and-coming local politician. Each of his siblings was attractive and accomplished. Story lines evolved, twisted and turned with the introduction of each new character or crisis. In those days, I lived in New Jersey near the border with Pennsylvania and endured two hour commutes at either end of my day. My body had slipped into anemia and with only 6 hours of sleep at night, I was burning out, despite being in my early 20's. I was however learning some Gaelic terms and numerous Old Country sayings and folk stories that neither my Irish born mother nor Grandmother had ever heard in Ireland.

The thing about working at a network as a "Vacation Relief" temp in those days was, you could never be sure when your workday would end. Crew guys assigned to one show, who had seniority with the network and union, could usually count on a regular schedule. They would be given just enough sweet overtime to keep them from bitching. Virtually no television production work was anything like your basic 9-5 job but some of the morning and afternoon shows came close.

During one afternoon taping of "RYAN'S HOPE," I was handed a message from Network Crewing. After we were finished shooting, they wanted me to report back to our main production facility. Unsure what to expect, I took a cab to 66th Street and Columbus Avenue. There I joined up with a production crew headed to NBC where we were told to cover the party for the ROBERT F. KENNEDY MEMORIAL TENNIS MATCH. The event was scheduled to take place in NBC's storied Rainbow Room. Crosstown traffic was brutal, and we were late getting to 30 Rock. We offloaded our equipment and headed to the elevators. Neither the Production Manager nor anyone else on the crew was known to me.

We set up in the lobby area just outside of the elevator doors. Other media were already there, busy recording members of the extended Kennedy family, invited guests, and notables as they arrived. It was certainly an impressive crowd with Camelot's queen Jackie O and Ted Kennedy presiding. ABC would be the only media allowed into the party because our powerful Sports Producer, Roone Arledge, was "tight" with the Kennedys." Or so he thinks he is," as a production assistant quipped to me... politics and egos.

A representative of the restaurant announced that only ABC would be allowed to record the actual party. Ted Kennedy came out of the restaurant and walked slowly through the lobby, a pace allowing camera crews to take their photos and record him. I had been occupied hitting on the daughter of New Jersey's Governor, with no success. You can't kill me for trying! Kennedy spoke with reporters, smiled, and acknowledged the crowd while walking leisurely. Suddenly there was a surprisingly loud CLINK from an empty corner of the room... Kennedy immediately flinched. Apparently two empty champagne glasses left casually in the sand of an ashtray fell together and created the sound. When you are the last surviving male member of a political dynasty and both of your older brothers have been assassinated, you quickly respond to unexpected sounds. The sad legacy was all there in his instinctive reaction and in his eyes. I'm sure he probably routinely checked out wherever he was staying or walking, who was where in every room, never knowing for certain. Safety and self-preservation were always situational.

The same restaurant representative returned and notified the crowded lobby that all members of the media and press would have to leave now except for ABC. We were now free to enter the party. As the other media packed up and left, the ABC people filed into the crowded dining room. It was a high energy ensemble with celebrities and notables gathered in chattering groups of 6 around the luxuriously set tables adorned with fresh flower arrangements. Jewels and beautiful faces shone in the soft, flattering light. Some guests entertained the table with anecdotes of the well off and famous. Others hovered cheek to cheek passing along gossipy tidbits and hot scandals to hungry ears. It was one of THOSE groups, a grazing ground for PAGE SIX and lesser outlets that feed off the crumbs of the Luminous, turning conjecture to fact and the most casual of momentary side by sides, into blazing romances. Tonight, I was a very low-level part of the ABC pack.

Our camera guys worked the room quietly, concentrating on recording the famous and connected, at ease and play. Oleg Cassini hugged Jackie O while her estranged sister, Lee Radziwill watched Jackie and plotted revenge. The entire group of Kennedy kids, Ted and Joan Kennedy, the widow Ethel, and so many more were there. We worked for around 45 minutes. Then the unusually considerate Production Manager invited us to relax and enjoy the party while she awaited further instructions.

I set off to find the restroom, worked my way as unobtrusively as possible between the tables. Even the busboys were better dressed than myself... my day's plans had never included hobnobbing with Kennedys. As I was trying to transit the room, Ted Kennedy chose that moment to cross in the opposite direction. Our paths met behind one of the tables and as Ted squeezed by me, I placed my hands on his shoulders to let him know the proximity was ok. I felt the smooth silky texture of his well-worn tuxedo. Then two hands slid around my waist, and I was staring into the smiling face of the Hollywood actor Cliff Robertson who had played JFK in the bio pie PT109, based on Kennedy's WWII heroics. He was just letting me know that he too was passing. I was the cut rate lunch meat in this celebrity sandwich.

About this time a warning light flashed in my tired brain. The message was, "HEY NUMB-NUTS... YOU HAVE YOUR HANDS PRACTICALLY AROUND THE NECK OF THE LAST SURVIVING KENNEDY BROTHER. MAYBE YOU SHOULD TELL THE SECRET SERVICE GUYS EVEN NOW REACHING FOR THEIR SIDE ARMS THAT THIS ISN'T WHAT IT LOOKS LIKE."

I snatched my hands back, almost clipping Robertson in my urge to disengage. I let both men pass me without further contact. Taking the PM's suggestion that I relax and enjoy the party, I grabbed a drink, filled a plate with some food and after finding a table where only one woman was seated, inquired if the seats were open. She invited me to sit. We began a conversation. She didn't recognize me, and she knew everyone. When I revealed that I was an ABC cameraman, I expected her to immediately realize that she needed to be somewhere else. She did not do that, nor did she suggest that I leave. She was much older than myself, very well educated, each word of her speech polished to a pearlish brilliance before being laid in front of me.

The more we spoke and laughed together, the more attractive she became and not because I was drinking. Meanwhile, I kept looking back over my shoulder to make sure our equipment was still visible. That meant we were ok time wise. My new friend revealed that she had been nursemaid to ALL the Kennedy brothers, from Joe Jr. to baby Ted. She had helped raise each of the boys and I suspected that she knew them better than even Rose, the snooty Matriarch of the clan, who had her hands full with the Kennedy sisters. I told her that JFK was practically a god like figure in our Irish-Sicilian family, right up there with Franklin Roosevelt and Lincoln.

My friend was conversant, charming, and surprisingly flirtatious. Believe me, I had turned the charm on until my personality controls were flashing SYSTEM COLLAPSE and "OMG preserve SOME dignity!" Her sincere interest in and acceptance of me was utterly unexpected. To be treated as nearly an equal by someone of her worldliness and experience was overwhelming.

After an equipment check, nothing had been moved, I happened to glance over at the dance floor and saw that Caroline was dancing with a partner. She looked radiantly happy and very much into the celebration. When I casually remarked to my friend how happy Caroline looked and what a good dancer she was, my wonderful confidant must have misunderstood me and thought I had suggested I dance with this Princess of Camelot. "Let me introduce you to her. She'd love to dance with you... she's VERY down to earth!" Although I tried to explain to her that I was technically still working and, on the clock, that should my boss see me dancing with Caroline Kennedy, she might have an issue with that... my friend had already begun to rise to go over to Caroline, I did another equipment check. Everything was gone! The rest of the crew and the Production Manager had left while I was occupied flirting. No one had even missed me!

After thanking my friend and sharing a quick hug, I bolted from the room, grabbed an elevator to the lobby... loading dock access was no longer an option... then ran out of 30 Rock, around the corner and down the lowest level ramp leading beneath the skyscraper. I arrived at the van in time to load the last box of stuff. No one had missed me. The Production Manager didn't question me at all. Now there was another problem. It was after 1:30 AM and I had missed my train back to New Jersey. The kindly PM must have seen the panic on my face and asked me what was wrong. When I explained to her what had happened, she activated her clunky stone age mobile communicator and booked a room for me at a hotel. I was stunned into silence by her generosity and caring. A cab dropped me at the hotel. I had no luggage, just the clothes on my back. The clerk gave me a once over appraisal, reluctantly handed me my key and pointed to the elevator bank. The PM had booked a suite for me... a luxury I had never experienced previously. The rooms were immense, with so much space and so many bedrooms that I went around shutting doors and leaving lights on just to feel more comfortable. I brushed my teeth with my finger and emptied out my pockets. There in my loose change was a shiny Kennedy half dollar which had somehow come into my possession without me noticing.

I lay on the wide bed literally meant for royalty and presidents. It was the 21st hour of my remarkable day. The experiences replayed through my sleepy mind as it struggled to make sense of the events. It was almost as though I had careened around on a TILT A WHIRL, been flung off and landed on this amazing bed, itself designed for the wealthy and pampered. The exhaustion caught up with me and before the front desk had properly entered my 7am wake up call, I'm certain that I was fast asleep.

MY FIRST KISS

Gene Simmons stood looking down at me with eyes as dark rimmed as a demented raccoon which had swallowed 2 hits of my cousin Kevin's homemade Blotter Acid. He held out his hand, offered me something, intently watching my reaction. The crowd pressed against the stage and screamed "TAKE IT... TAKE IT... GIVE IT TO ME!" I reached for his hand.

On the previous day we had been working together with his band at a recording studio in Midtown Manhattan. Gene fronted KISS, a bar band from Long Island, New York that had parlayed outlandish costumes and kick ass rock and roll into Platinum. Soon after we met, the band would become one of the most popular music acts in the world. That morning however, they were still in their formative stage and had arrived at the studio in their street clothes. After a brief look around at our recording equipment and the stage, the band vanished into the Makeup and Hair Departments. I don't think any of we mere mortals were prepared for the Beings that emerged a couple of hours later. Looking like aliens recently arrived from some very hip and outlandish quarter of a very stoned wider Universe, they towered over us in their high heeled platform boots. We had unknowingly been privileged enough to see them in human form, just four talented but anonymous musicians from suburban New York. They had morphed, courtesy of skin tight spandex, garish make-up and other theatrical elements into this menacing ensemble. Their faces had slashes of makeup like vivid scars partially concealed by shoulder length hair. They seemed to be all spikes, sharp edges, and protective bits of armor like warriors from a Dark Ages European hit parade.

We were slated to record a straight forward music video. At that time these short pieces were meant to play in rotation on MTV and other music platforms. They were comically simplistic when compared with the elaborate, Hollywood style, big budget productions that were yet to come. Those would have well known film Directors and Art Directors, elaborate staging and even choreographers. KISS was still refreshingly just head banging, gut punching rock and roll.

Following the standard sound check we went on to record "CHRISTINE SIXTEEN" several times. Three passes with the entire band were done first. The band members walked gingerly and a little wobbly in their thigh high boots. They watched playback to decide if they were happy with what we had shot. Once it was agreed that we had gotten a pass they could accept, we then shot it again with the camera ops concentrating on one or two of the band members. This was done four times, once for each of the musicians, in order to give the editors lots of exciting angles to choose from as they assembled a video worthy of the music. The images of the montage needed to be as quick paced and exciting as the music. It was also vital that each band member receive adequate screen time and numerous obligatory close ups.

Eventually the band, the family members, and friends who had accompanied them that day, as well as the band's agent, the Video Director, Audio Director, and Technical Director were all satisfied. We were wrapped. Our tech guys put the cameras "to bed" and the band's roadies tended to the musical instruments. I overheard the band's agent order the head roadie to, "Make certain that Ace makes it to the concert tomorrow!" There was a implied "DON'T FUCK THIS UP!" to his insistence and concern. Ace Freely, the band's lead guitarist and number one bad boy, had a reputation for being both too stoned to perform and the one most likely to miss a recording session.

On day two we gathered at the legendary Studio 54. The former haunt of fashionistas like the notorious designer Halston, Liza Minelli, Andy Warhol's gang and assorted "beautiful people," Studio 54 barely resembled its former self. Not a shred of notoriety and impropriety remained. The nudity, bowls of cocaine, blowjobs and assorted other sexual couplings in the gloomy upper tiers of the theater were long gone. The frenzied attempts of outsiders and commoners to gain entrance were no more. It had become that most pathetic of urban things, a formerly fashionable venue, person, or thing that had become passé, lost its pizzaz and appeal. It had become just another Midtown location. Crowds of KISS fans now lined up outside of the already packed theater. The crowd within was standing and restless with excitement. This was a major accomplishment for them to get to see their idols perform in a comparatively intimate space. The band was already capable of filling arenas with their many thousands of seats.

Our concert was going to be broadcast live to Italy where the band was also popular. The video and audio crews were in place. KISS itself was ready to wow their European fans but there was one large problem - No Ace! Despite the Road Manager's stern warning on the previous day, the band's flamboyant lead guitarist was a "no show." Our show's Director was frantic, the Producers were apoplectic, and the Stage Manager was being ripped a new rectum as though he was somehow complicit in the guitarist's absence. The expensive satellite was whirling its way through space and obediently approaching its rendezvous with our little production. There wasn't a fan large enough for this shit to hit. The hour of broadcast was approaching as rapidly and as assuredly as the satellite. There could be no delay, no second chance. The European control room was a bedlam of Italian slang and profanity mixed with mangled English. In each of these very expressive and colorful languages the question of the moment was "WHERE THE FUCK IS THAT ASSHOLE ACE?"

At last, there could be no further waiting. KISS walked onstage and detonated an explosion of screams and yells. My position was on stage, next to Gene. It would be a lightning-fast show, just a few songs including their massive hit "ROCK AND ROLL ALL NITE." The remaining three members of the band played with all the exuberance they were famous for. Simmons' unnaturally long tongue made frequent appearances emerging snake-like from his masked face. Someone somewhere must have wondered who the invisible lead guitarist was, where all those fiery licks were coming from but no one asked. The last song was done. The crowd pressed against our stage with feverish determination to get closer to their heroes. Gene motioned for me to show him my hand. I opened my palm, and he pressed his guitar pick onto it. He then jerked his head toward the frantic fans, a look more grimace than smile crossed his ghoulish face. This surprising exchange was witnessed by the front rows who howled and pleaded for the plastic pic, knowing that before my filthy hands had fouled it, Gene's fingers had blessed it. When my eyes returned to the audience it was a mass of raised hands motioning and grasping, of screaming, smiling and pleading young faces. Not wanting to witness the melee that would surely come next, I threw the pic into the writhing group and turned quickly away. The band began yelling "Ciao," the Italian word for goodbye. Then Paul Stanley, the other spokesperson for the band, yelled "PUPPY CIAO!" the name of an American dog food. It was an inspired ad lib that undoubtedly amused the Italian fans but probably did little to make up for the missing Ace, who never showed up.

THE JOHN EDWARD SHOW

O ne of my favorite episodes of THE TWILIGHT ZONE concerned a con man traveling in the slightly less wild west. His con was his professed ability to call the dead back from the beyond. Many of the skeptical locals had made a great show of mourning for deceased loved ones. The stranger offered to exercise his "powers" and ease their suffering by having these lost loved ones return from the grave. At first a few of the mourners were pleased by the prospect of being reunited with their dead. Then reality set in. A henpecked husband considered how quiet his life had been since his wife's death. The bartender had cheated his late brother out of the jointly owned bar and had no desire to confront his vengeful spirit Eventually, the town's mourners paid the stranger NOT to end their suffering which was the grifter's plan all along. This being a Rod Serling script however, there was a twist at the end as the self-satisfied charlatan rode his wagon past the town's cemetery as its residents were rising from their graves.

In 2000, I was offered a spot on a Sci Fi Channel show built around a Psychic Medium named John Edward. Despite my doubts about his authenticity and prospects for the success of the show, I accepted. My first surprise was meeting John and realizing what a sincere and generous man he was. He came across as very genuine, as much in awe of his abilities as we crew would soon learn to be. This was no Alister Crowley looking to harness the powers of light or darkness in order to assert personal control over others. John related the information he received as an acquaintance would pass along gossip or a recent conversation with a mutual friend.

At first my belief was that most of the bereaved guests would probably want to contact the famous and notorious. There was however not a single request to connect with Houdini, John Lennon, Caligula, Mata Hari or any other notables. What the show's guests desired instead was one final connection to the wife who needed to make a quick trip to Walmart, or the child who had come down with a fever at a friend's birthday party or the 16-year-old driving back from the beach on graduation weekend. Such simple errands and everyday situations which resulted in heartbreak, mourning, and more importantly, no closure. Every grieving soul in our audience yearned for that chance to say goodbye or express their love, one last time.

John knew already that supplicants do not hear from the famous because there would be no way to validate any private information. With not even the most casual connection to the living, neither John nor the guest would be able to confirm any messages received. Confirmation of contact was of the utmost importance to John. It was that simple. Skeptics and media critics immediately attacked the show and John's abilities. He was accused of tricking guests into revealing personal information during pre-show interviews.

The skeptical accused him of eavesdropping on conversations as guests were sitting in the audience, "mind reading," deciphering body language, observing facial tics and other non-verbal mannerisms for hints and clues. Some suggested that the microphones placed overhead were intended to pick up conversations. Had anyone asked the crew we would have gladly explained that the microphones were omnidirectional and only good for laughter, applause, and crowd noise. Johns staff was too small to do extensive interviews and he couldn't possibly examine his 200 hundred or so guests individually to memorize their individual body mannerisms or use other sleight of hand mentalist tricks. We knew that the guests he selected to "read" were chosen at random and we accepted that it wasn't John doing the choosing.

If they had asked the crew, we could have told them that although we all liked John personally, we were withholding judgment on his "psychic" abilities. There was no love lost between the crew, the show's other Producers, and the Sci Fi channel. We would have picked up on any duplicity early on. We were seasoned professionals who had "pre-recorded" live shows and segments, worked on love scenes between actors who hated each other, taped faked "accidents" for blooper reels, and other elements of fakery and falsehood. That was all a part of the job. John, his "gift" and CROSSING OVER were an entirely new experience for us. We were protective of him even if none of us could explain his process or abilities.

Each of us had already seen and heard things on the show that were profoundly moving, experiences that we accepted as real and sincere. Sometimes tears do lie but not generally when they are your own. Most of the crew freely owned up to crying more than once. Next to war correspondents and political reporters, I would wager that your average crew of TV freelancers is a pretty tough bunch. None of us had any vested interest in John's career. The Sci Fi channel was not a valued client. Any of the crew people were free to leave at any time. We had no reason to suspect that the show would have additional seasons. We were there simply because we liked and respected John. Just as importantly, we trusted him. Most of us had brought friends and family members to the show, adding their names to the guest list. I gave my invitees assumed names just to dispel any doubts. Had we ever encountered any activity we thought suspicious, improper, or shady we would never have exposed loved ones to any reading or subsequent exploitation. Almost all of the crew had been read. Dante Pagano, another of the camera operators, had been read by John so often that guests recognized him as he arrived for work. John told Dante things that had happened at his home that day, while he was at work, incidents that Dante's wife confirmed later. Only one man quit the show, due to the religious convictions and concerns of his wife, who credited John's insights to "the devil". John had told the man things about deaths in his wife's life, that she had almost forgotten about and never shared with

21

her husband. Admittedly it got spooky at times. When John "read" any of the crew people, it was basically "off the clock," meaning that we were free to allow the Producers to use the reading or not, however we felt. Of course, John would read us regardless of how the other Producers felt about the delays. Another of the camera operators, when he realized that John's information was for him, requested to be read in private and off camera. John freely consented while everyone else had to sit and wait. Trust me, TV productions did not stop for crew people unless he or she literally dropped dead. Even that was sometimes not the case. On one famous soap opera, a cameraman friend of mine, Les, died of a heart attack during a five-minute break. The Producers put out a call for a replacement. The cast and crew walked off the show. Les would have appreciated that!

Skeptics immediately claimed the show was all a set up and since we were employed by the show and ultimately John, we were "In" on the scam, an entirely untrue suggestion. John was never anything less than gentle and respectful of the guests he read. No one was victimized. How can someone claim to speak with the dead anyhow? It isn't logical and scientifically impossible. What could the deceased tell us that we would be prepared to hear, understand, or believe? What would our loved ones say to us if they could communicate? That is the first quandary. John admitted that the messages he received were not always from those we most wanted or might reasonably expect to hear from. They were often from distant and forgotten friends, relatives we never knew we had or even utterly casual associations, such as the guy who drove you to the studio. In my case it was from a high school student with whom I had attended class. We weren't even on speaking terms then. That did not stop him from checking in with me 54 years later. John did not receive or relate messages or information that could not be validated in some way. Very often, the things revealed made no sense to the reading. These were given to whomever was read so they could confirm them later, by checking with family, friends or simply by remembering. A very frequent occurrence was the dual surprise when the grumpy husband "chauffeur" patiently waiting for his wife to be read, privately complaining that this was all bullshit, discovered that the reading was actually for him. Don't let it be said that the Spirits had no sense of humor. John also admitted that the dead did not "speak" to him as we might think. They showed him objects, spoke sounds, the information was fragmentary. People we seldom ever heard from in life had no reason to disturb us now. Small talk, nagging, or disturbing comments from those we had buried and mourned would undoubtedly cause personal and societal chaos, so for the most part, were avoided. Most of us have a hard enough time relating to and dealing with those still a part of our lives. Not hearing from everyone we have lost was a necessary form of Cosmic Fail-Safe Control. We could not deal with death in any other way. Messages related to John were primarily intended to reassure survivors of the continuity of caring, love, and consciousness. Our personal sex lives and when or how we went to the bathroom had no interest to the deceased. Free from jealousy, prudery and desire, without physical bodies, those issues no longer mattered. If John did not literally "speak" with the dead, what were the messages he received and how could he make sense of them? This is going to be a real flight of fancy but perhaps it will help to understand what might be going on. John's psychic ability and NASA space probes, which are electro-mechanical versions of our human sensory systems, explore the unknown. Territory that was at once familiar: rock, dust, terrain, but utterly alien. Maybe John's abilities and those of other legitimate "mediums" are to connect with and explore experiences that exist beyond separation and grief, the familiar as well as alien, such as the experience of death. Space probes and John's insights both communicate in symbols, images that neither John nor the probes understand. The recognition of the meanings contained within the computerized data and the cryptic messages that John received were meant for others to decipher, interpret, and utilize.

For both the probes and John their roles were simply to receive, collect, and convey information. Just a guess on my part but arguably as good as any other explanation. Perhaps the domain of death is as close as the thoughts in our brains, the beats of our heart. The lightyears separating the planetary bodies have been calculated. The distance between life and death might be as narrow as a sigh or more vast than space and time.

Unlike many psychics, John never tried to claim personal control over his abilities. There was no pretense to either his full understanding of his gift nor any suggestion that he could direct or harness the Spirits who had given it to him. He was always very careful to abide by the rules they had set down. He often said that violating their trust meant possibly losing his contact with the afterlife. It sounded reasonable enough to us anyhow. On each day of production, the standard procedure was for an assistant to walk through the entire office and studio with a smoldering bunch of sage. This had been used by Native Americans as a purifying agent, to chase away evil spirits. John relied on it also. Media critics suggested that everything reeked of marijuana smoke and that we were all stoned. Undoubtedly, they were speaking for themselves. When John received the signs, symbols, and sounds conveyed to him by the Spirits he would ask the audience if any of them recognized something as simple as, "They're showing me an envelope with an orange on it... Yes... it's an orange... and there is a dog jumping up at a ball... he's playing with it... and I'm hearing Al or Alfred... does that mean anything to anyone here?" Usually, he would be drawn to one of the three different tiers of audience... being pulled there by the energy, images, and sounds he was receiving. Sometimes no one would "claim" the reading. He would then ask the spirit for additional clues. Eventually someone would say, "John, I think that might be for me." Almost like a bingo game with everyone waiting for that one telling number or clue. Some guests claimed readings at the first clue and then John would have to delicately let them down if the Spirits kept urging him on. He was acutely aware, as were we all, that everyone in the audience was grieving, hurting with emotional, and even physical pain. We all needed to respect their needs. If a guest insisted the reading was meant for them, John would ask why? If their answer was, "Well, I love oranges, we had a dog named Al who liked to bat balloons around." It was often that simple a connection. Then the taps would open, and other revealing and more pertinent thoughts and memories would come through. By now, the poor recipient would be quaking with emotion, crying and laughing at the same time while a friend or helpful audience member took notes on whatever John revealed. This went on for hour after hour. The afterlife had nothing to do with the length of the sessions or our schedule. He read guests until the afterlife was done with him, regardless of lunch time or breaks. He read until everyone he was meant to read had received the information they were meant to hear. Should he receive information that no one claimed, the show would stop until someone acknowledged it was meant for them and claimed the reading. Trust me again, this most DEFINITELY never happened on other TV shows. On one occasion John was literally stuck for nearly 15 costly minutes as he insisted that he was being drawn to a corner of the studio where there was no audience. No crew or studio workers were anywhere near that part of the room. Unable to proceed, John asked a PA to go into the building next door to see who was standing around near or in it. The structure was a parking garage and the PA returned with a thoroughly overwhelmed, confused, and nervous man. He parked cars there. John explained what he was doing and asked the man if the following bits of information meant anything to him. He was seeing a waterfall, a teacher and a drowning. It was a tropical setting. The man began to cry. He was Jamaican and had been a teacher there. He was swimming beneath a waterfall with his younger brother, who drowned. The surviving brother had always assumed the blame for the accident. He had not forgiven himself. John said, "Your brother says you were not to blame for his death. That you should not feel any guilt. That he loves and misses you." The poor man was an emotional wreck. He was escorted to the grief counselor who was always on the set. Whatever you might think, this was about as far from ordinary television as my career had ever taken me. Our average audience was primarily middle class, dressed in various kinds of black garments, they smoked, too much and lived in Long Island. If there were any university professors visiting as guests, they kept the information to themselves, unless they were "read" then the intellectual defenses and pretensions melted away. One such couple had lost a child to disease. The child's spirit contacted them through John, using the names of relatives and information the youngster could never have known. The parents collapsed into each other's arms, reassured that the spirit of their child had not simply vanished.

One reading was particularly memorable for me. After John established that the reading was for a young woman, John said "It's your brother... he's thanking you for dancing with him at your wedding. Why is that so unusual? It was your brother, and your wedding. Why wouldn't he dance with you? I'm confused." The young woman was weeping as she explained that her brother, with whom she was exceptionally close, had been killed in an auto accident just before her wedding. Initially she wanted to postpone the event, but her family encouraged her to proceed anyway as that is what the brother would have wanted her to do. On the day of her wedding, she removed his photo from its frame and pinned it inside her wedding dress, not telling anyone for fear they might consider it morbid. So, she danced all night with her brother, even if he was only there as a photo and in spirit.

Don't ask me where these things came from. We heard such stories several times an hour of each taping day. We observed grief wracked people finally understand why they kept finding feathers, seashells, or other talismans around their homes that had associations to deceased loved ones. These insignificant everyday objects were meant to remind them of the presence of benevolent and caring spirits, still a part of their lives.

As we worked, I watched John's face for hours. I saw him become impatient with both Spirits and guests who refused to cooperate. Some guests only wanted to hear from some special person directly. John would have to remind them, "Forget who you came here wanting to connect with. They may or may not come through but so long as you do not acknowledge and accept whichever spirit is trying to reach you, I will be blocked... then no one will get through!" When he was able to make a solid connection, with the spirit providing easily recognizable information and the recipient catching on quickly, John would smile with pleasure, sharing in the guest's happiness. He genuinely wanted people to experience some relief from their pain, some reassurance. He also understood that these were mere quick fixes, spiritual band aids on wounds that only time would eventually heal, or not. In more extreme cases, therapy would be needed. He was doing what he could, fulfilling his mission and his life's work. The stories of dead children were the hardest for us. The raw pain on the faces of the parents, their faltering voices and sobs, shattered us. We knew that these also stressed John out more than any other of the readings. Children simply should not die before their parents. It was unnatural, unforgivable. John attempted to provide no reasons for such tragedies. He offered no platitudes or references to God's awful plan, merely the possibility that loved ones remained aware of and cared for their survivors. His only evidence was the intimate personal information conveyed through him, a complete stranger. The names of meaningful objects, nicknames, pet's names, oddities of dress, favorite songs, the remaining shards of shattered and broken lives known to only the deceased and their survivors. It was something at least, small consolations, but perhaps they carried more weight than homilies and sermons.

While we were in production, 9/11 happened. Overnight there arose a tremendous need for contact with missing loved ones. An impossible need that no one, no organization or group could minister to with so many dead, survivors left with nothing, no closure, just an aching void. The Sci Fi Channel wanted John to do a "Special", that disgusting corporate need to monetize anything, even disaster. To his credit, John refused. To the individuals who contacted him for private meetings he had to tell them that none of the spiritually traumatized dead, who had passed violently, would be ready yet for making contact. Even the dead needed time to heal, recognize what had happened, and understand and accept where they were. John trusted that once the Spirits were ready to make contact, he would assist as best he could, but not for broadcast. One afternoon while we were taping, and I was shooting John on my camera, my phone buzzed with a call. Once the Director switched to another camera, I gave my phone a quick look. The number was unfamiliar to me. I let it go. The next day while we were recording and John was the subject of my camera shot, my phone buzzed again with the same unknown number. After the taping I called the number. A recording revealed it was a non-working number at a bank in the Financial District. Confused now, I called the number's prefix and four zeros. A man answered. I explained to him that my phone had been receiving calls from this number. After a long pause, he said that the number was non-working, that the place of its origin was no longer there. I asked, "Was it by the World Trade Center?" After a long pause he answered, "No." My impression was that he was not being honest and instead obeying some corporate mandate to not give out information, especially to strangers. Non-working phones in vanished offices don't make calls. Years ago the bank had been among my clients. I knew people who had worked there at that time. Had they moved on, retired or been lost? I would never know.

Just before leaving John's show there was one last personal experience for me. My wife had her mom and two sisters visiting with us. When my car pulled into our driveway late on that Sunday afternoon, my young son bolted out of our kitchen door wearing his

Superman costume. Its cloak flapped around behind him in the late afternoon light. It was a wonderful sight. At dinner, the three sisters and their mom talked about their late father's birthday, which was coming up. That Monday was my return to CROSSING OVER for the week's shooting. I wondered if my wife's father would make an attempt to communicate. It was his birthday after all and the four most important women in his life were gathered at our house, which did not happen often due to geographical separation. The thought remained in the back of my mind as we worked our way through the morning. The grief and loss we were exposed to on any ordinary day of taping was so overwhelming that most personal thoughts were forced into insignificance. John was searching in the audience section to my left for the person he was being led to. My camera lens framed him as he paced to and fro in front of the anxious guests. We had been asked long ago not to claim a reading for ourselves unless we were certain it was intended for us. This left fewer annoyed guests and critics ready to pounce on anything they thought might prove collusion between John and his staff, people it was assumed he knew very well. I was not paying particular attention to what John was saying until he mentioned seeing a young boy in a Superman costume, in a bright light. No one claimed it. Despite this very particular clue, I waited for that one last bit of information that would confirm my hopes and suspicions. "I'm seeing the number 18," John said. That was our street address but as I mentioned earlier, EVERYONE was waiting for that longed for reading. As soon as John said, "18," a woman yelled "It's for me John... it's for me!" and began to sob. I could tell by John's face that he seemed unconvinced that the reading was for her but since no one else had spoken up namely ME, he began to read her. Audience members desperately wanted contact with deceased loved ones and would sometimes "hijack" a reading, forcing bits of information to fit their narrative like you would shave a piece to make it fit a puzzle. It takes otherworldly energy and determination for the Spirits to break through into our chaotic and distracted brains. I immediately regretted my timidity. It would have been a wonderful gift to my wife and her family. The father and husband had died long before his daughter and I met. If it had been his spirit which had managed to get through the formidable barriers between our worlds only to have me not answer his "call," I could imagine him thinking: "Stupid bastard... what did she EVER see in him?"

"CROSSING OVER" eventually ended its run. John went on to write more books, podcasts, personal appearances, and private readings. When one of the other camera ops on our crew died years afterwards John attended his funeral. He's that kind of guy. As far as my friends on the crew and I were concerned, he was and is the real thing.

MISS BETTE DAVIS WILL SCREW YOU NOW

1987

Barbara Walters was ABC Network's prima donna news lady. She was the very first Prime Time anchorwoman in American TV history. She still had "glass shards" in her puffed-up hair after shattering that Glass Ceiling. There was no love lost between she and the male Anchors. Although she persevered and made inroads, I don't think anyone was happy with the situation. I was working at ABC then and would often be assigned to local or Evening Network News.

My dear friend, Jim Tomlinson, was a Production Manager at ABC at the time and Barbara's interview show was one of his productions. I was freelancing by then and the Network seldom used us on their productions. Jim was trying to get me onto their production crew hiring list. Their staff cameramen despised us and thought freelancers were after their jobs. They were correct but we had time on our side. The Network eventually threw most of their staff to the wolves. We got the work in the end. Barbara's guest for this interview was legendary Hollywood bad girl Ms. Bette Davis. Ever seen a photo of Bette laughing? Or even sincerely smiling? No and with good reason. This woman not only knew where the bodies had been buried in Tinseltown, she had helped to put a few of them there herself. Ms Davis had survived feuds with other female stars, shitty marriages, deceit, backstabbing, and that soul gnawing insecurity and jealousy that seems to accompany every signed studio contract.

Jim had hired me for the gig and just asked me to keep a low profile so the staff guys wouldn't get unnecessarily irritated. When I worked as a freelancer at the network studios, the staff guys would sometimes sabotage the equipment to make our job more difficult. We usually warned them that sooner or later they would be freelancing also. Eventually, the staff camera operators were bought out, sent fishing, or to early graves. Staff who had worked full time for many years could not always adjust to retirement, earned or forced. Freelancers like myself were more used to intermittent employment and had learned to start side hustles to bring in earnings whenever we were between shows.

My honest opinion was that working with Ms. Davis would be an honor, a career highlight. She was one of the very few survivors of Hollywood's Golden Age, celluloid royalty still alive. Davis was the textbook example of feisty. This remarkable woman had more sharp edges than a yard of razor wire. She could cut as cleanly too and with about as much emotion. Although age had mellowed her considerably, I knew that I would need to be completely "on my game!"

I was a new addition here and not part of Barbara's regular crew. Someone's buddy, boyfriend, or relative might have lost work for me to be there. No one would have my back except for Jim, and he was also a relatively new comer to Barbara's team. Insecure and guarded after decades in television, she felt most comfortable with people she trusted. New faces were suspect. Barbara and I had worked together many times at ABC. Yet she would have had no idea who I was. Network camera operators were interchangeable; we rotated from show to show so talent seldom felt any need to relate to us. Most didn't bother.

It had been a tough year for Ms. Davis. She was still recovering from a stroke, a mastectomy, and a hip replacement. These health issues had probably muted her legendary crankiness. I'm sure she took private pleasure from having outlived her enemies, former competitors, and 4 ex hubbies. All the fights were over and not only was she still standing, she was being interviewed as a name and person of interest still in demand.

Bette sat in her interview chair, staring off into space. She had incredibly thin fragile legs inside patterned black stockings which made them appear stronger and more fashionable. She was wearing an attractive robin's egg blue dress and matching eye shadow. She sat there with the bored and impatient look of a passenger awaiting an overdue train for a trip she really did not want to take.

She watched the room and production people with appraising looks... taking an interest in someone... watching them move and then abandoning them for the next subject. The woman had a fierce gaze, and I could only imagine what she must have looked like in her heyday. She stared at faces and clothing, the decor of the room. Some things she commented on to no one in particular. Most of the time spent waiting she sat in an icy, brooding silence. No one from the production team was attempting to entertain or distract her. Everyone on Barbara's team was fully occupied dealing with our temperamental Host and her abundant needs. Since no one knew me, no one felt obligated to speak with me. I must have had the same look on my face. My expected place was behind my camera and that is where I stayed. Ms. Davis and I sat in silence, just two outliers.

Barbara traveled with her own makeup and hair team. The Lighting Director was her guy also. She would allow no one else to light her. The many lights set up in the apartment size room soon made the trapped air uncomfortably warm but if Davis had an opinion about the heat, she kept it to herself. Her singular complaint was that the snow on the runway at Orly Airport in France had delayed her flight to New York.

She opined that the Producers were lucky they had decided not to conduct this interview in Germany due to the generally horrendous weather plaguing all of Europe. She referenced her trips there as one might casually describe driving to the local mall. Not world weary exactly, but worldly. An experienced traveler to whom the world was now merely a list of favorite hotels, restaurants, and friend's neighborhoods.

She seemed to pay particular attention to me because we were the only two outsiders in the living room set. Both of us were ignored in the flurry of activity which swirled around us but still managed to leave us untouched. Since even the Stage Manager, whose responsibilities included catering to the talent paid her scant attention, I stepped into the void. Before I was a cameraman, I was a Stage Manager and a goddamn good one too. I thoroughly enjoyed keeping talent comfortable and involved with the show.

Ms. Davis was drinking from a pewter goblet which I took to refill. She had been drinking a lot due to the heat. As I carried the goblet back to her, my fingers left smokey impressions on the chilled metal.

She had begun to smoke cigarettes in succession, as she was impatient and possibly a bit nervous. The interview began. Bette chatted up the room. She related stories as things came to her mind, moving from one subject to the other. She was enjoying herself. Barbara, by comparison, was stiff and humorless, too self-aware of how she appeared on camera. It was almost as though Ms. Davis had overthrown that studio-nurtured tyranny of the importance of one's looks to one's career.

Barbara was self-conscious, fidgety, and rigid. Her inescapable anxiety made her speech harsh and sharp; charmless. She seemed totally incapable of spontaneity. The unexpected unnerved her and made her uncomfortable. When I worked with her and co-anchor, Harry Reasoner, I used to watch him stare at her with cold malice, as though willing her to fail. We all knew he not only hated sharing the news Anchor position he was especially annoyed that it was with a woman. That studio set was sometimes an uncomfortable place in which to work.

Whenever we took a brief break, Barbara's "glam squad" of makeup and hair would descend on her like corner men at a prize fight. They did everything but wave towels to revive her. I took Bette's glass and refilled it. She stared at me appraisingly, as though deciding whether or not to say something to me. Thinking to be helpful, I quietly said to her, "Ms. Davis, is there anything else I can do for you? Anything you need?" After coldly looking me up and down she responded in a super loud commanding voice, "YOUNG MAN, I'll TAKE YOU SOMEWHERE PRIVATE WHERE WE CAN BE ALONE AND I'll SHOW YOU WHAT I NEED!" So much for keeping a low profile. She had delivered the line without a smile or hint of humor.

The entire production staff, crew, and Bette's escort began to laugh, including me, although my embarrassment was easy to see. I think she might have been as surprised at her comment as we all were. Ms. Davis smirked slyly. She still had it in her to WOW a room! I don't think Jim was expecting his "new guy" to be propositioned on set by a famous film star. He looked at me, winked, and shook his head no. I imagined him saying, "I know you're a dog but you wouldn't, right?" He did not seem very assured.

Meanwhile, Barbara heard the convulsive laughter and since she had not said anything funny, nor heard anything, she froze. Then in a panicky confusion said "WHAT HAPPENED? What did I miss?" Once the incident had been explained to her, she seemed amused in spite of herself. It would be a funny little anecdote she could share at some Upper East Side dinner party.

The interview was in conjunction with the release of a book Bette had just published. The book was an attempt to clear her reputation of the harsh allegations raised in her daughter's book about their mother-daughter relationship, or lack thereof. Bette was settling scores right to the end. She died two years after this interview.

PORN

"IT ISN'T ME... I'M NOT FARTING," yelled the thin blonde. She was wearing a transparent teddy and white panties. On the front of her underwear was printed a yellow traffic sign with stern black letters announcing "ENTER HERE." There was a similar traffic sign on her ass announcing, "TWO WAY TRAFFIC."

She was as self-righteously aggrieved and insistent as a woman could be while standing in her underwear in a room full of strangers. The show's Director, as exasperated as his indignant young star, tried to soothe and appease her by saying "I know honey, we know it's not you but the sound seems to be coming FROM you, uhhh..from BENEATH you!" "FUCK YOU," she screamed and raced back into the impromptu dressing room. The door slammed. She refused to open it for the Producer. The shoot was at a standstill.

The Director walked over to the sound man sitting in a corner, hovering over his Nagra and equalizers. Bending close to the bearded man, who slid his headsets off, he whispered, "Is it her? Is she farting?" The technician seemed a little embarrassed at having to seriously answer this unlikely question. "I don't know. I mean I can't be sure, but it SEEMS to be her, the young blonde!" The Director next asked," Is any of it usable... anything we shot? The harried man replied "Not the fart parts... I mean, it's really fucking audible someone's letting 'em rip!" The Director sat near me and mumbled, "What the fuck. What the hell else could it be? Is it the host? Just what I fucking needed today. The blonde can endure a 40-minute four way with no problem but can't sit still for a fucking 30-minute interview. FUCK!"

The hostess was a minor television celebrity well known to be easily offended and fiercely vindictive if she felt insulted. Even carefully asking her if she was responsible for the rude sounds might provoke the "real thing"... a veritable "shit storm" and certainly end the shoot for good. Let me make it clear that I don't work on porn. Clients offer me shoots and I take those that sound interesting and fun, or let's be honest, shitty and miserable if I'm hungry enough. Any port or studio in a storm, right? I did have standards. No oil companies, military or fly by night rock and roll producers who would vanish after the shoot, leaving us with worthless personal checks.

I had no idea that this shoot would be "soft porn." Isn't "hard" the entire point of porn? But whatever, there would be lots of female nudity, some dancing to crappy disco music, no penetration and probably not a cock in sight. At least that was what I hoped. It was just another job in Manhattan working with people I did not know and would never see again. It was not so much a job as a mortgage payment. When considered in those terms, nearly anything was bearable. Thankfully, New York City was not known as a hub of porn shooting activity.

Having arrived early for the shoot, I had set my camera up and then sat in another room, waiting for our stars to exit the wardrobe. The location was adjacent to a dorm used by NYU students. The dorm rooms were surprisingly dark for late morning. The reason became apparent when the white brick walls were suddenly aglow with the exaggeratedly enlarged shadows of women undressing. One could easily follow the progress of the strip tease just by watching it unfold against the screen of brick and dark windows. The women lowering their jeans, tops flung away with bras and long legs stepping out of panties. I soon suspected that somewhere in those dark rooms lurked hyperventilating lower classmen who had skipped class for this particular lesson.

A man sat on a sofa near me. He resembled Elton John circa his CAPTAIN FANTASTIC days, with long stringy blonde hair falling from beneath a jaunty cap over indigo tinted glasses. He began a conversation with me, so I closed the book of poems I had been reading and turned my attention to him. This was very early in the day before it would dawn on me that this was not a regular "he said/she said" interview.

He asked me if I had seen any of the films our younger star had done. He recited a few of the titles, most of which involved home 'deliveries' by well hung pizza guys, a horny cable repairman, and assorted other workers. Then he spoke rapturously about her two most recent releases of "FORT DICKS" and "THE FLEET'S IN!" which its sole reviewer called "A patriotic penis party!" and "Nobody tops a mast like her!" rewarding each with four thumbs "WAY up!". By that point I knew what might lie ahead.

As he spoke, his hands cradled a mixed drink from the craft services bar, his fingers splotchy red and swollen white from the tension. That struck me as peculiar. The burlesque show continued beyond our windows. At last, the women were done with make-up and hair. They retired to a Naugahyde sofa and we began to tape. Together they discussed their careers, how to get around a booking when your period arrived, stars with body odor, bad breath, and the awkwardness of dealing with distant uncles who had seen their films and shot one too many lascivious glances their way when passing the corn at family dinners.

Suddenly, we heard the first fart. Everyone discretely ignored it, who doesn't fart right, albeit we are not usually being recorded. After a short pause there came another fart sound, unmistakable. This time the women shot each other a look, an undefinable moment passed between them in that quizzical "look." They resumed the sexual shop talk about guys who could not "perform" for very long. The young blonde laughed, wiggled on the sofa and there was an even louder and more distinct fart. "CUT," yelled the Director.

The stage manager gave everyone a five-minute break. The women had returned to their dressing rooms. I sat and read. There wasn't a job that I accepted that didn't find a book or two in my backpack. On film and video shoots there are often long stretches of down time dealing with wardrobe issues, blown lights, or other problems that interrupt schedules. It's one thing to sell my time and another to have it wasted for something beyond my control. That's why books always accompany me. Most Producers tolerated it and if they didn't, they could find another cameraman.

The women returned. They had way too much makeup on which made them look like dolls, but it was currently the look everyone wanted. They began to discuss their films. The younger girl was still in the early stages of her career. Our hostess, to use a colloquial expression, had way too many miles on her, but it was her show. The young blonde was particularly proud of her most recent release: "THE FLEET'S IN!" In this direct to DVD film, she cavorted with three buff, bearded sailors, indulged in some mild S&M rigging and made nearly believable moans as she worked the sailors' masts while all four of them were carried along on a wave of lust; oh boy. The women laughed together, rocking in their seats and then WOW... the fart sound brought our progress to a complete stop.

"Cut," yelled the soundman. The Director immediately ripped into the poor technician, giving him a lesson in TV set etiquette and just who was able to call "cuts." It was a very short list and did not include soundmen. The technician retreated in silence. We had all distinctly heard the sound. We suspected that the issue was a very distinctive gastrointestinal problem being suffered by one of our guests. The Director then bellowed "CUT!" and called for another five-minute break. I opened my book and resumed reading.

Now it developed that my reading habit had been observed by everyone on the set. That I seemed more interested in my poetry than I was in the nude women sitting so close to me. A court of a different kind had been in session and a verdict had been passed: I must be "playing for the other team!" It wasn't that I had no interest in females, just not in these two.

Following another aborted attempt to resume recording the interview and more apparent bouts of flatulence, the Director yelled, "CUT... CUT... WHAT THE FUCK STEPHANIE... SHOULD WE BUY YOU SOME BEANO?" Sensing the mood in the room and realizing that it had not been her, the blonde shot upright and began screaming, "IT IS NOT ME. I'M NOT FARTING. IT'S THE FUCKING SOFA!" She stormed into the dressing room.

I was just as confused as everyone else by the dilemma facing the production. All we knew was that we could not continue with recording while awaiting the next fart. Our extremely limited progress had stopped dead. This time I wandered over to the craft services table and poured myself a cold drink. The loft we were shooting in had become very warm, heated by the lights we were using and the number of people in the small space. The AC had been shut off so the editors would not have to contend with the sound as they edited the piece at some time in the future.

My palms were sweaty, my shirt damp and clingy. My brother's wife used to rub their daughter's skin with baby powder whenever it was irritated or sticky with perspiration. Perhaps the actress was innocent after all. We returned to the set. Taking a chance, I suggested to the Director that maybe the young woman should consider rubbing her legs and thighs with talc to make them smoother. The Director merely stared at me. Mentally I began to steel myself for the expected harangue of "ONLY ONE PERSON MAKES SUGGESTIONS ON THIS GODDAMN SET." To my surprise, the anticipated rebuke never happened. Instead, the Director asked the Makeup and Hair people if they had any baby powder to rub on the actress's legs. They did, it was liberally applied and the young woman was asked to sit on the imitation leather sofa again. The Director instructed her to move around. The obedient girl squirmed, rocked back and forth, slid forward, slumped, crossed and uncrossed her slender legs... not a sound! No fart noise; problem solved! Then everyone turned to look at me. I could almost hear their thoughts, "The guy with the poetry book knew this trick that none of them had heard of before. He has probably shot so much porn that this is nothing to him. He's a porn pro. God only knows what wild, kinky, revolting things he has not just watched but also shot! From the looks of him he undoubtedly participated in the post shoot activities... Jesus... what a pig... probably gave the camera a virus just touching it!" The Director thanked me, never asked the name of the poet I was reading and threw quizzical glances at me for the rest of our shoot, perhaps watching me with newfound respect. We wrapped our recording gear. The Director thanked me once again, everyone left the loft and headed to other shoots in other places. I never mentioned to anyone that baby powder also works well on sticky doors, to cut the steel-on-steel resistance on dolly camera tracks and anything that needs to slide.

PS: the poet was Charles Bukowski!

DOING TIME

Dedicated to Ray Chiste

The burly prison guard grudgingly welcomed our five-men two-women crew with disdain. It was obvious we were the last thing he wanted to deal with that day... a goddamn documentary television crew. Like meat to hungry lions, and we had females on the crew too, Christ! There was a time when they would not have allowed women inside the prison, but times had changed he must have thought. Pure bullshit.

"Don't wander," he warned us. "Ya need sumthin' you ask, we get it. DO NOT GET CLOSE TO THE BARS. DO NOT!" As he spoke, we looked around us at the faces of the multitude of prisoners yelling, hooting, and whistling at us. The women were being deluged by requests for sexual favors and promises of how satisfied each of these guys could make them. The complete catalog of sexual act was proposed and shouted out. There were growls, moans and the acrobatic wagging of starved tongues. There was some laughter among the other mayhem makers as the Lotharios attempted to one up each other with their offered services. Our females were definitely rattled but kept their cool. A couple of the prisoners just stared, said and suggested nothing. they were the scariest of all. In truth we were all nervous. Joan, our English Director, stood her ground. In her "Swinging London" days she was known as "Joan the Bone." She laughed at the vulgarities and took the sexual invitations in stride. It was far from just another day for any of us, but we felt confident that at least for our brief stay here, we would be safe. We only needed a few interviews. After the inmates saw that we were not intimidated by their verbal assault, they became bored and returned to walking around within their cells. I saw one of the girls and a couple of the guys were shaking but they continued with their respective tasks. As we began to record, the murmur and noise subsided. The men had begun to listen to one of their own speak about himself. For this, they were respectful. Even the guards listened intently. We heard the usual references to childhood want, physical, emotional, and even sexual abuse. Everyone knew we were the "bleeding heart" kind. We didn't have to believe what we were hearing... separate truth from deceit... just record it. When Joanie was satisfied that we had what we came for, we packed our stuff up to a soundtrack of renewed sexual suggestions. My attention was caught watching one of our crew wrap an electrical cable around his arm. He had absentmindedly stepped closer to the wall of bars than he should have. He was laughing as he looped the cable, flirting with a female Production Assistant. Greedy eyes watched him, envying his freedom, hungry for opportunities of their own. One of the prisoners was giving him a predatory once over and I felt certain that he was just awaiting an opportunity to grab at the guy through the bars. I asked the girl and guy to give me a hand with something, which moved them beyond the reach of the inmate. The prisoner then switched his attention to me as though I had taken something from him, deprived him of something he had already begun to consider rightfully his.

On the following afternoon we journeyed to upstate New York to a county work release security facility. We were the same crew. Inmates were given the opportunity to learn a trade here, to assist in their transition to parole and getting a new start on life. Unfortunately for our peace of mind, the inmates were learning to butcher meat. Sharp knives were everywhere. The gender of our two crew females was of much interest to these men. No bars separated us here. I kept imagining that someplace within the hierarchy of the New York State Penal Authority, some bureaucrat was having a laugh at our expense. All of us were relying on the good sense of these prisoners surrounding us, this mix of races and ages handling saws, butcher knives, and cleavers.

They rough housed, cursed, and kidded with each other. A rainbow of colored tattoos covered exposed arms, hands, and necks. The next victim needed to be chosen. A prisoner walked me around the pen where the cattle were kept. The stink of fear and death must have unnerved the animals. Some snorted and bumped against the fences while others stood quietly, waiting. The inmates chose a large steer which was herded into our area. Isolated now, he watched me with large, watery eyes. In a futile attempt to perhaps lessen his fear I ran my hand along his hide although I doubted that the touch from any human hand would fool any of these doomed animals. He had a metal, numbered tag stapled to his ear. I began shooting the process. With the camera on my shoulder, he was just an object within my lens. This helped me to feel removed. The animals' eyes were wide with fear; slobber hung from his pinkish nostrils and lips. My hand on his wiry coarse and dusty hide kept me steady.

Snorting and complaining, hooves clopping against the concrete floor, he was pulled forward. An inmate with a bolt gun waited there and as the animal's head came close, he fired once and the large animal collapsed onto the floor. Chains were attached to one of its legs and the carcass was hoisted up onto a conveyor belt. The huge beast was cut open and its insides spilled out in a splashy whomp and whoosh, falling into a metal receptacle. Now the inmates set upon the still warm body with their knives and saws. The legs were severed, body splayed wide, hide removed and the usable bits of meat separated from the offal. The process went quickly. The men were well trained.

After only a few minutes of shooting I handed my camera off to my assistant and walked outside for fresh air. There beside me was a drum holding numerous pieces of cattle. On top was the skin of this last steer, I saw the same metal tag still attached to the severed ear. In mere minutes the animal had gone from a hulking, snorting mass to what could have been a Halloween cattle costume, steaming in the chill air.

While working at my first TV station, the PBS Producers decided to do a public interest shoot in the Trenton State Prison. It was an old, maximum-security facility and held the state's only electric chair. The inmates had nicknamed it "Old Sparky." A stage had been set up in one of the exercise yards. Every surface in the yard was bare. There was nothing on the walls or floor. It was monochromatic and monotonous. Security was very tight. Every tool and cable we brought in and had to be accounted for, each box opened and searched. Guards like it when there is no change to the daily routine. The inmates are volatile by nature and my guess was even they preferred things to stay the same day to day. Sudden change was disruptive and opened doors to problematic behaviors and made everyone "nervous." You don't want nervous prisoners or jumpy guards. We had been assigned a trustee to show us around and lead us to our lunch in the cafeteria. We ate with other inmates who watched us with a mixture of interest and perhaps envy. We could walk out of there that afternoon, go for a beer and pizza, drive to the shore, get laid. Our possibilities were endless, and these men knew that. Every one of our camera crew had gone to college and no matter how brave we felt we kept any swagger concealed. We neither belonged nor fit in here. Two of our camera crew were Black men but we all sat together. The inmates were divided by race, by choice. Our prisoner trustee was a talkative guy. Friendly and informative, he had even offered to show us the electric chair, but we declined.

As we sat together over our trays of bland institutional food, the trustee soon melded right into our little group. We shared laughs and jokes. He offered the chips he wasn't going to eat to us. We were relaxed despite the presence of so many prisoners. One of our crew asked him what he was in for. It seemed like an indelicate query no matter how innocently it was expressed. Then our new friend casually mentioned that he had inserted a raw two by four plank into his wife's vagina and kicked it into her body until she hemorrhaged to death. I'm pretty certain those of us who had not been politely watching his face as he told his story were more than happy, we had been staring at our shitty lunches. Right then and there I realized that murderers can be exactly like us, indistinguishable, common and ordinary. It was as though a cloud had passed over each of us and left us suddenly not as sure of the world or the people, we shared it with. I tried not to imagine what the wife might have looked like and just hoped she had been mercifully drunk or stoned during the attack. I already knew what she saw in this man. She probably never suspected the homicidal rage that lurked behind the charm, quick smile and easy laugh. As we returned to the yard for rehearsal, he stopped us in front of a thick metal door, its single tiny window barred, steel ribs laced across its white surface. "That's where they keep the crazies... they NEVER let them out. There's some spooky mother fuckers behind those doors... they'll never see daylight again!"

The concert went well enough. Our cameras had been set up on risers and we were surrounded by prisoners. seated lower than us. I avoided making eye contact with any of the men. They spent as much time watching us work as they did observing the musicians. My friend Ray Chiste was wearing a new pair of expensive sunglasses. I overheard one of the men say to him "Hey, I like your shades... give them to me." it was said as a command. I glanced down once and one of the men threw me a kiss. We were only too happy to wrap our gear out of there once the show was over. Any one of us could have left the oppressive atmosphere of the prison at any time during the day. We were the lucky ones. Employed, with some security and reasonably bright futures. We had the option to quit our jobs, break leases, buy a car on credit and drive to wherever the roads ended. We had choices good and bad, control over our lives. Without even knowing it, we had escaped.

BIG CATS

There is a period during that stretch of time between the cold nights of winter and steamy evenings of summer during which Floridians congratulate themselves for living here. We can switch off the air conditioning and sleep with open windows. Nature co-operates with cooler nights and warm, breezy afternoons. At least for a few months the suffocating humidity that the state is known for is absent.

We mark the change of seasons by the sudden appearance of the various colored license plates of "Snowbirds" arriving to escape the cold and snow of Northern latitudes.

It was the onslaught of COVID 19. My days were spent holed up in my home. Nearly all TV production had been put on an indefinite hold. My vacation rental calendar was now a mess of "sorries" and cancellations. I had the leisure to read a book from my library, expand the garden, or just think about isolation, pandemics, and wonder what might come next. There was now ample time to binge watch television programs that looked interesting or recommended to me by friends whose critical judgment I trusted.

One such title was "JOE EXOTIC," a Netflix series about a flamboyant hillbilly conman. Gay, fond of fringed jackets, guns, and big game tigers, he was also adept at harvesting runaways, young studs, and women whose personal roads ended at the bus station nearest to Joe's private zoo in Oklahoma. From among these desperate and luckless people, which included convicted felons, the addicted, abandoned or otherwise lost, he chose his zoo employees and four husbands!

The series was just the latest disturbing snapshot of contemporary American culture. It seemed to cover most of our national obsessions with guns and the desire for celebrity status, dreams birthed in the mire of ignorance, greed, and eccentric passions. The series had it all, with doses of mayhem, treachery, and violence. The least threatening characters were the enormous tigers and lions themselves.

The only salacious aspect missing was the usual discovery of hidden graves and bone bits. Mercifully, Joe didn't kill any of his gay partners, despite his fondness for discharging firearms. None of the former sexual gay drifters were fed to any of the 100 plus jungle predators kept in his compounds. With our country's terrible history of serial killers, this was a wonderful relief. Joe's enclave was only one of an archipelago of similar private collections, sketchy zoos and dubious sanctuaries for animals stretching across America. Despite the popular enthusiasm for laws protecting animals of all kinds, these enterprises continue to exist and flourish. There are approximately 4000 tigers alive in Asia, India, and Africa today. Here in the United States, it is estimated that there are between 5,000-10,000 big game cats in captivity. Certainly, not all were obtained legally. Local officials themselves might not even be aware of just how many of what kind of animal are being housed within their jurisdictions.

Around 1984, my good friend Warren approached me with an offer from friends of his who lived in Bucks County, Pennsylvania. They had their own tiger sanctuary set amid the colonial era villages, tract houses, private estates, and state protected swaths of pasture and agricultural land near my then home in Lambertville, New Jersey. Bucks County, named after William Penn's estate in the UK, is primarily a bedroom community for professionals commuting to jobs in Philadelphia, New York City, and Trenton. Despite the county's rapid development, if one of the tigers did manage to escape the sanctuary, it might be able to elude recapture for longer than might be expected as there are still tracts of heavily wooded land. An overly abundant number of white-tailed deer would prove to be an ample food source. Local drivers would certainly appreciate fewer roadside collisions with the animals, whose mangled carcasses lined local roads.

The couple wanted to produce and market a video about Siberian tigers or perhaps approach a television network about doing a special. Warren wanted to know if I might be interested in shooting and editing such a program. I was "between shows" as freelancers liked to say when we had not worked in a while and had nothing much coming up. I agreed to meet with the friends at their animal compound. Warren was a hustler like me only in a different business. He was a graphic artist. We were both very familiar with check-to-check finances, doors opening and closing, promises unkept. Our ships never seemed to come in.

I had just been released from ABC. Warren was managing an art framing place at a mall and writing pornography on the side. Despite being an imaginative writer of all things sexual, he was flummoxed trying to write a piece for men obsessed with licking women's toes. Since each perversion has its own designation, these afficionados of toe jam were known as "shrimpers." I am sure you can guess why. Irish, bald, bearded, and able to look up at a Leprechaun, Warren was talented, impish, and possessed a very vulgar wit. He eventually became a minister, of course.

Warren picked me up and together we drove along tree shaded back roads which wound through rocky hillsides, between sunny fields, and over a couple of single lane wooden bridges. During the surprisingly long drive, he filled me in on what to expect. These tigers were Siberian, the largest of the big cats. Known for their strength and ferocity, they even hunt animals as large as black and brown bears; let that image sink in! They can stalk, surprise, kill, and consume bears.

According to Warren, the average Siberian male tiger is around 9 - 10 feet in length, weighs up to 600 pounds, and stands four feet high at the shoulders. The average female is 8 feet long. Their tails alone can be 3 - 4 feet in length. They can easily outrun humans and climb trees, which I had been wondering about. You know, just in case! A tiger named Jaipur, raised in the United States, grew to over 12 feet in length and weighed over 1000 pounds, just like the cats I was expected to work with. The couple had an arrangement with the local road crews. Whenever a deer was struck and killed, a very frequent occurrence, the crew would bring the bodies to them. Dead opossums, rabbits, and the occasional hawk or crow would be thrown in. The Big Cats preferred to hunt and toy with their prey, but I guess will scavenge other remains if the body is not too decayed. This deal with the road crew saved the couple money and the guys a drive to the dump with a rotting carcass. Everyone was happy with the arrangement.

Eventually we turned onto a narrow, rutted lane and followed it to a ranch style house. Beyond the house was a heavily fortified and fenced series of enclosures. From this more secluded, wooded area came a deep roar. A welcome perhaps? Warren had told me his wife and toddler child could not accompany us because his wife was having her period and the scent of blood might "agitate" the tigers. The young child might look like a possible meal. Duly noted.

The husband and wife came out to greet us. They went into more detail about the program they were hoping to produce and sell. My part in the process was to direct, shoot and edit the piece. I had the free time and was up to the challenge, so far, so good.

We walked to a caged enclosure where the tigers lived and were able to enjoy a limited run. This was attached to a wide, fenced area much larger than a yard but still able to be surrounded by a high metal fence. The yard had a few wooden structures for the animals to climb on and hopefully amuse these creatures used to roaming for many unobstructed miles. The Siberian tigers are solitary hunters.

As we walked toward the caged area, the tigers paced and moved constantly, watching us with what I hoped was only curiosity. They are apex predators with no natural enemies. I found myself imagining what these massive, restless animals were thinking, what they smelled, and what their hunter's instincts were calculating as they watched us approach. I glanced at Warren, not much taller than his son, whom he had been advised not to display to the tigers, a man size meal even if a little gamey! One of the tigers suddenly rose on its hind legs and stretched out huge, padded claws, not attempting to climb the fence; not exactly anyhow. Nevertheless, I was very thankful for the extra metal mesh extending beyond its reach. This was fully 9 feet of tiger rearing up, flexing its strength and power.

The husband told us the tigers had already been fed so they were in a playful mood. He suggested that I enter the enclosed yard and he would allow the animals to leave their penned area. I think he wanted to observe how I would react to the tigers and just as importantly, see what the tigers would make of this strange human with the smell of Aqua Velva?

The security gate swung open for me to walk inside. I noticed that none of the other three people were intending to join or accompany me. Was this to reassure me or the animals? The door closed and locked behind me.

The tigers were massive faced, masks of curiosity, and stood together as they watched me enter their area. The husband slid the locking bar open and several of the beasts padded out immediately. I couldn't determine their individual gender, not that it mattered. Who cares what color the car was that hit you, right?

Was there any rivalry between the cats? Any questions concerning dominance which might be quickly settled with the quick killing of one slow moving, overweight, out of work cameraman?

Tigers are "Free Agents." Freelance predators, unlike lions which hunt in groups known as Prides. I stood rigidly still and tried to quell any tell-tale whiff of fear that my body might unconsciously radiate. Thor and his wife had cautioned me to make no sudden movements or run. Tigers, like all cats, can be very affectionate and playful, if in the mood.

I had seen enough cat owners with lacerated arms to know that the animal's tolerance of affection and human companionship can change rapidly. I'm a dog person and had always considered a cat's loyalty to be pure self, totally one sided, and iffy, at best. Why would anyone pay for, feed, and keep an animal that at any moment might rake your skin with its claws if it happened to feel like doing that? Entirely too much discretionary freedom there for my taste. Hell, human moods are hard enough for me to gauge. I'm a dedicated fan of the family dog, even if despised by some for the animal's servility. It loves people, will die for them if necessary, and follow owners to their graves, if permitted. Cats? Once they've eaten and used the litter box, everything else is fair game, especially birds, young rabbits, and any stretch of exposed human skin within paws reach... preferably that of their owners.

The three tigers circled me. One rubbed against my left leg. When a 400-600-pound animal rubs your leg, you bend it. The cat's head was as large as my chest, each paw as wide as my outstretched hand. The cat raised its head for me to scratch its neck; it was nearly level with my face. Suddenly, an unexpected nuzzle from one of the other animals pushed my body against the tiger I was already petting. I was now sandwiched between nearly a thousand or more pounds of predator. Playful mood or preliminary bump, like sharks?

The second tiger, after brushing against my left leg, sat and began to look at me, not directly, not with a challenging stare, more a casual "I'm not really looking at you, but you know that I am!" appraisal. The tiger sat there, its head higher than mine, just two apex predators chilling together, staring around at the hard worn dirt beneath us, waiting for what might come next. Thor had warned me not to stare directly at any of the animals as they might consider it a challenge. Once again, duly noted, but what is the protocol if the tiger stares first?

I stole quick glances at the animal. The hubcap sized mask of a face with its crazy fur tufts in Halloween colors of orange and black, opened its mouth to yawn. There were the 4-inch-long incisors, the largest of the big cats, its tongue as wide as my arm.

A million years of mutual hostility had been bred into us. Each creature taking turns hunting and being hunted. Had the couple raised the cats from cubs? Did they associate human scent with danger? Having recently eaten, how satisfied were they? Did any of them crave a dessert? An atavistic prompt from deep within my human collective memory urged "It's time to go. Show and tell is over!" After I left the enclosure, the tigers began to chase each other around the large space. My Siegfried and Roy moment was over.

When I rejoined my hosts, it was like a scene from a nightmarish petting party. "Wow, they really like you," said the husband. This caused me to wonder "Wait a minute was there a fucking chance they wouldn't like me?" I guessed I would have been the first to know. The color had returned to Warren's face. "They are really taken with you," the wife laughingly observed. Their spontaneous endorsements and assessment of the situation had entirely too much of the surprise to suit my taste. Had any of them been expecting any other reaction and if so, when was it my turn to learn the odds? Both comments were spoken as you would to a child who needed to be assured before petting a strange dog.

Once the feline meet and greet was over and predator introductions completed, the four of us returned to the main house where, over beers, the couple began to discuss the project in greater detail. I had successfully passed the audition, lucky me. What if I had failed either party? The couple thought that what would make their product better and more interesting than your average "ANIMAL PLANET" show was the fact that the big cats mated for 4 or 3 days, 24/7, with lots of roaring, snarling, and fierce couplings. During that time, all humans stayed out of the caged area, including the owners, a wise move.

This is where my services came in. Their plan was to construct a platform high above the open area, AKA, an official tiger mounting and fornication area. I would remain on top of the platform with food, water and a waste bucket and record as much of the sexual antics as I was able. Remember the info about tigers being able to climb trees, break spines and snap necks? I certainly did. I also figured that following all that rough sex might at least one of the tigers desire a little snack. Hell, it's not like they could enjoy a post coital smoke. An after-sex snack was a habit of mine, why not tigers? So, what if the odd smelling morsel had been inconveniently left on top of a platform? A little challenge might make it even sweeter.

My mind pictured the headline in the local news: "ADVENTURE SEEKING AMATEUR WEDDING PHOTOGRAPHER DEVOURED WHILE SHOOTING TIGER SEX ACTS!" On our return drive, Warren asked me what I thought of the proposal, and could a ballpark budget be worked up quickly? I was noncommittal. After a polite interval, I declined the opportunity to make animal documentary history, referred them to a guy who shot exotic two-legged animals engaged in similar activities and waited for the reviews.

THE OLDE COUNTRY 1989

"**Y**ou're more Irish than Sicilian you know... I was BORN in Ireland. Your father was born in Brooklyn. I crossed an OCEAN. He crossed a river!" This was my mom's opening salvo in an age-old family dispute... the Irish versus the Sicilians. My father just stared at her, appraising the assault. Mom reminded my siblings and I that the Sicilians had been conquered by everyone throughout their history, literally everyone with an army. Bullied by invaders from Europe, the Middle East, and Africa, they had never encountered a potential enemy whose ass they couldn't kiss or surrender to.

This was a frequent take no prisoners battle fought at the kitchen table, Riverdance versus the Risorgimento. Meanwhile, the Irish had saved Western civilization in Europe. They were fierce warriors, seldom conquered, unlike the residents of that other island farther to the South. While Mom and Dad went at it, we would concentrate on eating our Irish stew, spaghetti and meatballs, corned beef and cabbage, or pizza. Dad would simmer and then open up with both guns, "It's a goddamn wonder that the Irish even managed to breed. Ever watch them dance? Arms nailed to their sides, jumping and kicking with a few foot swirls just to keep the circulation going in their rarely washed flounder white feet. Christ, Hadrian had to build a wall to keep them out. They weren't even worth conquering... all filthy matted long hair, women with hatchets and blue painted faces... the country's main export is priests... PRIESTS for Christ's sake... an export you can't use for anything; you can't eat it or resell for a profit. Ever seen a thin priest?" Mom would respond, "It was the Romans who built the wall... not the Sicilians. They were too busy being conquered!" This re-stirring of the American Melting Pot's unmixed bits continued on throughout our youth and right into high school. Personally, I favored the tales of the ancient Greeks and the Romans making Sicily the empire's breadbasket. The descriptions of my grandfather's tomb robbing childhood, his memories of the scent of citrus blossoms, and taste of sweet wine, were more appealing than my mom's recollections of rain, constant cold, rampant tuberculosis, and religious bigotry. We managed to hold each heritage in equal disinterest, while still giving both of them the respect family roots deserve, even if our only real contact was a trace of brogue in the speech of certain older relatives. We kids made the cultural journey from Riverdance to the Risorgimento over many a meal.

My mom used to say that I was born with "gypsy feet," just another of the phrases and terms, like "Indian giver," we grew up with which are now four-letter words and banished from polite conversation. When I was a toddler, my parents used to play a game with me. They and their friends would take turns passing a hat from one to the other. Since I knew the hat meant that its wearer would be leaving, I followed the hat and would go to that person, expecting to leave the house soon. It was a source of great fun for the adults, but it must have blown my developing "gypsy" mind and gifted me with a healthy distrust of expectations. Perhaps my innate desire to travel was due more to my being the child and grandchild of immigrants; family members who had fled poverty and religious hostility to find a haven in America. We were raised hearing stories about the two fabled islands our ancestors had fled from. I longed to visit them one day, preferably on some other person's credit card.

My opportunity to travel to Sicily came eventually at my own expense, but one of my Sicilian relatives hooked me up with a tour company which made me an "offer I could not refuse," if I was willing to travel with a church group. I was converted but went my own way once we landed in Palermo.

Then in the late 1980s an opportunity to travel to Ireland materialized, this time with a television program being produced by the Catholic Archdiocese of New York. My position as the Director of Photography enabled me to choose my good Irish friend John O'Connell as my talented and affable video engineer. John and I had worked together on numerous shoots, often under stressful conditions and in rough locations. I could count on him. Our Director, Joan Wood, was another friend and storied survivor of the 1960s era, from London: she was also an actress and author. Her sense of humor was as ribald as my own. She could make and take a joke and had no trouble being a part of a crew, helping with whatever needed doing. Her boyfriend, Ray accompanied her. Ray was a gregarious, New York City homicide detective. Empathetic and quick to laugh he had just enough of an edge to discourage unnecessary bullshit, no matter its source. He manifested the world weariness and spiritual exhaustion of someone who has had more than a passing acquaintance with death unnatural and deliberate. A man who had rummaged for years through ghastly crime scenes in search of motives and means. Our final crew member was Father Pat. A balding and bespectacled older priest, gentle and bookish, who had probably never spent a day of his adult life, outside of a rectory or church. He had worked with Joan, John, and I before and was probably already preparing himself spiritually for the contests to come during his week together overseas with these minions of the devil, just like Fr. Merrinn in THE EXORCIST! We had already reached an agreement that when our speech, stories, or joking became too much for Fr. Pat, he would say, "Presence of God." That was his safe phrase and a reminder to the rest of us to calm down.

Father Pat would act as our "Spiritual Chaperone" and purse holder. Together the four of us left Kennedy Airport for the Emerald Isle. Except for Fr. Pat, we were a crew of hard living professionals, used to brutally long workdays, excessive drinking, mild drug use, and prone to vulgarity in all its forms. Our dispositions mixed well. The Diocese of New York wanted to document the experiences of Irish American immigrants; the who, why, and when of their journeys to the New World. We had already shot interviews in New York, including one with my mom.

We arrived in Dublin, then had to collect and document the many equipment cases we had brought with us. We had our camera, tripod, audio recorder, lights, cables, wires, and boxes of video tape stock... all awkward, heavy stuff. Everything needed to be inspected and checked at Customs and matched with the Carnet. Once the boxes had been loaded into our rental van, we set off to the religious community building where we would spend the night.

Since this was Ireland and the hour was late, nothing was open. We had been assured that we would have dinner waiting for us upon our arrival at the rectory, so we were not overly concerned. A priest opened the door, welcomed us in hushed tones and apologized that since it was well after hours, everyone was asleep. The place had the distinct smell of celibacy, which I remembered from my stint in a seminary studying to be a Catholic priest. My flirtation with celibacy ended up being more like a one night stand than a lifelong calling. The rooms were clean, nothing feminine anywhere nor any kid stuff obviously. Our dinner was waiting for us in the refectory. We respectfully followed him into the kitchen, he showed us the fridge and then bid us good night. Opening its door we discovered levels of nearly empty shelves, no leftovers of dinners past, or extra dessert. Yet there on an otherwise bare wire rack was our first dinner in Ireland; Slices of uncovered boiled ham, chilled slices of white bread, and a slab of butter or mayonnaise. We made ourselves sandwiches with no great enthusiasm.

We shared universal disappointment. This would not be our last poor meal in Ireland. Father Pat was staying at a guest house somewhere and had taken our vehicle. Trapped, hungry, and tired, we went to our respective rooms and lay upon the dog bed thin mattresses set upon metal beds with incredibly squeaky springs that protested each time I moved.

The morning's weather was cold and thickly overcast, AKA summer on the Emerald Isle. I was thrilled though, that Ireland was beneath my feet and filling my eyes, and that someone else was paying for my trip. Our first location would be the beautiful Trinity University. Fr. Pat arrived with the equipment packed wagon and picked us up. Our first interview was with a history professor who would narrate the story behind the massive emigration of Irish citizens to the United States. I set up my tripod and a few lights. John readied the Beta-cam. It would not record. Something was wrong with it mechanically. If we could not get the camera to work, we were screwed, and a long way from home. In a panic, we called Sony who could not troubleshoot the device over the phone. The next nearest Beta-cam was in Japan. They had not yet been widely adapted in Europe.

John began to fool around with the camera's guts, probing here and there with his mini screwdriver. At last, the camera responded as it should, loading the tape cassette placed into its side and was now ready to record. Thank God.

We were all freezing. My winter cold protection included thermal underwear, a thick wool sweater, parka, wool cap, and gloves. The local Irish guys were walking around in just open jackets over thin looking sweaters. How did they do it? They must get used to the cold and damp from childhood on. Even indoors we shivered. There did not seem to be a heating device or thermostat in all of Ireland! After Trinity, we packed our gear, carried the bulky road cases down narrow staircases, through venerable stone arches, and across quads to our wagon.

Our next location was a small church in a picturesque village. Curiously, a bisected statue of the crucified Christ lay against one of the exterior stone walls, the lower half missing. No one bothered to give us the background to the accident.

The verger opened the church for us and then turned on the electric heaters, which soon brought the interior up to a balmy 50 degrees. We recorded the parish vicar who discussed the flight of people who had left the villages following the Potato Famine, the broken families, failed and abandoned farms, suicides, and hopelessness of the local population unable to leave due to age, poverty, or infirmity. This particularly holy man was Protestant and wished to keep the north's ties to Britain. This religious conflict, like all such wars, just seemed ludicrous and irrational to us but then what is rational about religion? I thought again of the bisected Christ statue, a suiting metaphor for the utterly severed Christian religion.

In general, each of our interviews were running from 60-90 minutes. They would be edited back in New York after our return. Once we were done taping and had thanked the priest, I watched as the verger went around opening the windows to release that very expensive electric heat back into Ireland's frigid atmosphere. What was it with the Irish and their seeming national aversion to warmth? I had never felt such a Sicilian-American sun loving, comfort craving in my life. With a last look at the halved Savior, we set off to record some B Roll... pretty shots of grazing animals and the icy gray skies above green hills, before heading north to Belfast. That beleaguered city would be our base of operations for the rest of our stay.

My Mom and her family had lived in Belfast. Her ancestors had watched as neighborhood men were dragged from their homes and shot to death in the street while their frantic children watched. English soldiers or their provisional thugs, the Black and Tans, waged a war of terror in the Catholic neighborhoods. My great, great-grandmother used to carry ammunition in her shawl, ferrying it to IRA gunmen. My grandfather's plumbing shop had been burned down twice. When my mother was old enough to apply for jobs, office managers would unlawfully remove the applications of girls who had attended Catholic schools. When my grandfather gave up on having his own business and started working at a shipyard, he had been forced to jump into the harbor and swim to safety as gangs of Protestant workers, men like him trying to support their families, roamed through the shipyard beating Catholic workers with iron pipes and metal wrenches. Leaving Ireland was their only option.

With our cargo area crammed to its roof with large black canisters, tubes, and boxes, we set off for the drive to the North. It was not a great physical distance from Dublin to Belfast, but psychologically, it is immense. The border crossing went smoother than expected. We needed to show our passports and the official Carnet to the guards who were courteous. Ray's detective badge and Joan's London accent sealed the approved entry and we hastened on to Belfast central. At no time during our stay in either part of Ireland was our equipment inspected. In retrospect, it was my guess that the authorities kept track of us, and we were deemed non-threatening.

Our entrance into the North had been remarkably, even suspiciously easy. We had to remind ourselves that we were entering a recent war zone. All the fighting had been urban, so the countryside had remained free of shell craters, the hulks of burned cars, and other telltale detritus of warfare. Most of the scarring and damage had been psychological and borne by the residents of the riot torn streets and neighborhoods under siege. We were looking to get to our hotel as soon as possible. All of us ached bone deep from the damp chill that had surrounded us all day.

In those pre-GPS days, we were forced to drive through the unfamiliar streets of Belfast looking for an address. It would have been so much easier had someone told us to look for the enormous vibrantly crimson and gold Mandarin Chinese ceremonial gate that marked our hotel's driveway. This place would have looked garish in West Hollywood and might have caused a Scenic Designer to exclaim "Oh my God, have you NO shame?" Maybe in Hollywood, such a display of cultural appropriation might have been dismissed as tacky, but still acceptable. Perhaps there was a large Chinese Irish community in Northern Ireland. I never asked and not one of the very Irish desk clerks bothered to give any explanation. Perhaps a 20-foot-high Celtic cross rising out of an imitation neolithic Druid barrow would be as readily accepted in a Chinese neighborhood, but I doubted it.

The hotel room was clean but Spartan, absolutely no frills, with room heat apparently being considered not only a frill but a luxury. The rooms were like those of a third-rate college or Basic Training. The tile floor of the bathroom was so icy that when I walked on it in my double layer of wool socks, my feet left footprints of moisture, outlines of body heat. When my hand was placed on the radiator style heater, it was stone cold.

It was hard to accept but probably logical, Northern Ireland was even colder than the South had been. None of us could get sufficiently warm. We had yet to have a passable meal either, anywhere in the country.

So far, Irish food made English fare seem imaginative and succulent. Thank God for breakfast. This hearty and abundant meal not just started our day but needed to sustain us until dinner, wherever that unhappy event might end up being. To this day, thick Irish bacon has a special place in my artery clogged heart. American bacon needs to be called something else. At breakfast we all looked disheveled and groggy. It was obvious to me that at least a couple of the others had slept in their clothes also. None of them had heard the sporadic gunfire that I had heard. Father Pat had booked private accommodations in an upscale guesthouse. One of the perks of being the boss, or at least the one holding the Diocesan credit card.

We went into a Catholic neighborhood to record more B-Roll visuals. It was one of the areas from which many of the residents had fled. This morning we watched a 5-man patrol of English soldiers walk down the narrow street as children raced around with complete disregard for the very serious looking men. The soldier walking point, first in line, constantly scanned rooftops watching for snipers. The one at the rear of the patrol did the same thing, looking behind at the area through which they had already walked. Housewives stood and talked together; casting looks at the soldiers ranging from derisive sneers to outright hostility. No one spoke to the heavily armed men, who were uniformly young. Older veterans wanted nothing to do with this unpopular posting. My camera seemed to annoy them. I'm sure they already knew we were Americans working for the Catholic Church, and therefore hostile.

I had very mixed feelings watching the soldiers with their battle gear and undoubtedly live ammunition in their weapons. It was an incongruous sight. Tense young men dressed for war while surrounded by weaponless women and children. Not exactly an alien sight in our strife torn world, but these men and women spoke the same language, were of the same race, watched the same shows on the telly, danced and sang along to the same musical groups, yet were seconds away from wholesale violence and death. The laughter and yells of the heedless children which currently filled the streets and echoed between the rows of identical, attached brick houses could easily turn to screams and thunderous gunfire. Some things still don't compute and all because a headstrong English king wanted to get laid, and a scornful Pope refused to concede and look the other way.

In my household growing up, all I heard from the Irish, Maternal, side of the family was hatred for the English. According to my sweet natured, exceedingly generous Grandmother, they were Satan's Spawn. From Cromwell to the Royal Family, they were all butchers with blood-stained hands... perfidious, insatiably greedy, child killers. My grandmother's idealized Englishman was as masculine as the former Duke of Windsor, knit and wore monogrammed slippers, and resembled Marty Feldman, whose thyroid tormented "googly eyes" made him look deranged. Now that was English manhood according to Nanny.

My Sicilian-American father praised the English for standing with the United States through numerous wars. He praised their military resourcefulness and courage but complained they were lax about cleaning the blood off their warship's deck following a battle during World War II. Disgusted by this slovenliness, his American sailor buddies used to call them "pig boats". His admiration for all things English did NOT include the Royal Family. Those snobs he considered "leeches" sucking the blood out of the English treasury. One thing he did share with my wee English loathing Nanny was contempt for sad old Edward VIII, the Duke of Windsor, whom he considered a Nazi-loving coward. We shot very little on this sad street. We were interlopers in their war. We just wanted to peek, record a bit, and then scurry back to the safety of the good old stable USA.

Our next location was near the same area. We were to record an interview with a reputed IRA gunman who was forced to spend all of his hours and days in hiding, in the apartment provided to his family by the very government he was fighting. Somehow, he had ended up on the "kill on sight" lists for both the IRA and the local Protestant Provisionals. To venture outside of the apartment, even to drop by the neighborhood pub for a quick pint, would risk his being executed.

We arrived at the apartment complex where hundreds of families lived on the dole, with everything provided by the government. The buildings looked like any project housing I had seen in the Bronx, Newark and many other locations all over America. The area was littered with gutted automobiles, burned out lights, smashed windows, shopping carts, and spray-painted graffiti curses. Slogans praising the IRA were also prominent.

We unloaded our equipment and walked toward the Housing Unit. Here was more debris... discarded mattresses, broken chairs, and screen shattered televisions. We were not entirely sure which apartment our guest lived in, so we began to knock on doors. Invariably, a woman opened the chained door just enough to see what we wanted. Behind her were clustered ginger and blonde-haired kids in Catholic School uniforms, straining to catch sight of us, excitedly smiling at this much appreciated interruption to their homework time. If anyone needed proof that poverty is not racial, this was it. The moms were courteous and super friendly but kept the chain in place just in case. We opened our wallets and handed out 10's and 20's to these beautiful people, wishing we could help more.

We eventually found our guy and were welcomed into their small apartment. While his wife fretted that they did not have much to offer us as refreshments, the uniformed children sat and devoured us with their eyes, as if we had arrived in a spaceship. They stared as we set up the camera and a few lights, knee socked legs kicking excitedly. They were straining to sit still but wanted to know about EVERYTHING... until their mom shushed them into polite silence.

The room was heated by peat logs in a fireplace. If you stood directly in front of it, you might be able to warm your hands and face, but your ass would be cold. When we were finally ready to record, the man began to narrate how he had ended up a prisoner in his own home. Misunderstandings, misperceived slights, and the absolutely dreaded Irish accusation of being "an informant" had sealed his fate. He was a defeated and frightened man without purpose or support.

It did not take us long to realize that if he imagined or was told that if he granted us this interview, spoke honestly, and at great risk about his predicament, it might somehow gather him some assistance from Americans. Good Old America was always ready to right wrongs and defend the proverbial Little Guy, except that in our case it was mostly hype and bullshit. This interview might be seen, if it was viewed at all, by Sunday morning early risers, the sleepless, and shut-ins unable to switch channels. It was nearly impossible to think that anyone who might watch the show would either think or be able in any way to assist this man.

We packed in silence, each of the crew understanding the futility of what we had just done. Ireland was leaving us nothing but cold, from our frigid fingers to our aching hearts. After this interview, we drove to the notorious Falls Road Prison. A line of women, assuredly Catholic, remained on a vigil outside its walls. Each was hoping to pass along news about the family, parole hearings, advice from lawyers, or just hoping to catch sight of a longed-for face. This was the only location where we were asked to stop shooting. A plain-clothes policeman roughly suggested that if we did not comply, our equipment would be impounded, and we could face charges. Even Joanie's magical London accent cut us no slack here. We reluctantly moved.

Our final location was at a club which the local government of Belfast had established for teenagers. Probably, an attempt to keep them from falling under the influence of the IRA. I sincerely doubt that it accomplished anything close to that goal. The club house was situated in a repurposed building, perhaps a garage, in an area that had been the site of much sectarian fighting. It fronted onto open land right in the middle of the city. There were around twenty-five teens and older kids there when we arrived. Unlike their American peers, these kids were actually thrilled that someone cared enough about them to conduct interviews. At first, they wore masks of street toughness that gradually fell away as they talked excitedly about their lives, families, the struggles, and other pertinent subjects. Often talking over each other in their urge to be heard, they responded frankly and honestly to Joan's questions, unfazed by her English accent. The American TV show "A TEAM" was blaring away on their television set. It had not been shown in the States for a long time, but these avid fans watched it religiously, it was new to them.

They all had family in the states. They mentioned cities like Boston, Chicago, and New York with the same wistful respect that others show to El Dorado, Hogwarts, and Oz. The idea that family members in the States might actually see them on American TV was captivating to them. Their shared dream was to get to America themselves, someday. But between landing at JFK and this clubhouse, there were unresolved and frightening impediments. They had no jobs nor little expectation of finding one. Wages were low, drugs plentiful, and the English and their Paramilitary allies were a constant threat. None of them were packing to leave just yet.

Joan called for a break while the kids relaxed, she could check her notes. She knew Ray would need a smoke, and I would appreciate some fresh air. Before me was a wide field, bulldozed clear of the rows of houses and stores that had once been there, an entire slice of community scraped clean. Perhaps my mom's birthplace had been among them, this was the part of Belfast she said she was from. The field was dark and despairing, an anomaly in this crowded city, a void. Glass shards glinted from among the scrubby weeds and pulverized brick. Once again, I was forced to remember similar urban scenes in Detroit, New Haven and other American cities.

About three quarters of a mile away, an English helicopter gunship hovered noisily over another part of this devastated field. Beyond that, a wall of attached brick homes made a boundary of sorts between the living and the dead.

The wind swept the sounds of the gunship's rotors to me, their ceaseless roar was intimidating. Predatory searchlights poked from the ship's sides and funneled bright cones of cold bluish light onto the fields, searching and probing for objects of interest. A lone figure walked along a distant pathway worn through the dark expanse. It appeared to be an older woman carrying shopping bags in each hand, making her way carefully through the darkness. A funnel of harsh light had settled on her, surrounding her small form. She did not slacken her pace but continued with her burdens. I wondered what would have happened had she panicked, dropped her bags, and run. Would the gunship crew just alert one of the many area patrols and intercept her?

Would they think her response suspicious enough to warrant a more drastic measure?

At first it had occurred to me that perhaps the copter's crew was lighting her path, giving her a generous assist, until the brazen beams darted away and settled on another place or person of interest in another corner of the flatland, leaving her to navigate the rest of the pathway in the dark. Now I was the tallest object on that nearly featureless flatland and since those hungry searchlights had not discovered me yet, I returned to the club house. We hugged the kids goodbye, avoided responding to their excited queries about when this would air in America and would it play on the BBC or Irish Television. While John and I packed up the gear, we played some of the interview back for the kids whose large eyes and happy grins shone in the monitor's glare.

Exhausted from the days of running around, loading, unloading, and carrying our gear, we had dinner and then returned to our hotel, the Ice Palace. I cannot remember any dinner we had during our stay in Erin, but I believe that was because the mind tried to protect us from misery and unpleasant memories. We ate something, somewhere, period.

That night the room was already losing the paltry amount of heat it had somehow managed to accumulate during the day. The radiator was still warm. Stripping the mattresses from both beds in the room, I made a shelter of sorts. My hope was that whatever wisp of warmth that might yet leak from the radiator. With one mattress as the wall and the other as the roof, I covered the floor with blankets, sheets, and mattress protector... any fabric that might provide insulation.

Sometime during the night, my hand touched the radiator and nearly adhered to it, frozen into place. It was just as stone cold as the previous day. I didn't even want to leave my little fort in order to pee. Somehow, my soul retraced some atavistic path through hundreds of past lives and ended up deciding that I would need to add more leaves and branches to the floor of my cave. And that, my dear reader, is the goddamn truth!

Once again, I heard automatic weapons firing deep in the night but no one else on the crew had heard it. Thank God, Belfast was nearly wrapped. Just one location left. We were a scary group at breakfast... overtired and severely under-slept! John had been plagued all night by the rambunctious partying of a rugby team that felt the need to celebrate all night. When John called their room to ask them to please take the noise down a wee bit because he needed to get up early for work, a hostile Northern Irish voice slurred into the undoubtedly spittle covered receiver "FOOK OFF YA AMERICAN WANKER!" then the phone was slammed onto its cradle. Immediately after this cryptic exchange, the volume of noise rose and John resigned himself to this new misery, shivering beneath the thin blanket.

We had one more location to locate. Once we were wrapped, we could make the return drive to Dublin and Aer Lingus to JFK. For this taping, we had somehow picked up a local assistant and guide. Someone in Brooklyn probably knew someone in Belfast, who had a friend, who had a daughter that might like to work on an American TV show that no one would probably either see or remember. Maybe she was supposed to be our interpreter?

She was a young woman and had obviously slept in her clothes. She projected the same confrontational attitude and a veneer of toughness that all the local youth did, courtesy of living in a war zone. Her arms were inked with crudely drawn tattoos, one of which was of the IRA symbol. There was no doubting her politics. She approached our wagon with cautious curiosity and looked at each of us four men, probably judging our intentions. She might have felt some relief at seeing Joan sitting in the passenger seat. We must have passed inspection because she climbed into the vehicle and introduced herself. Work is hard to come by in the North and she would be paid something for her time, we all hoped anyhow. Our trouble began after Joan introduced herself and the skittish girl heard her distinctly London accent. "HaIIo... you're English?... Jaysus" Our assistant was already apprehensive, worried that she had been seen getting into our car. In Belfast, prying eyes were everywhere, recording and reporting what they witnessed, or thought they had seen , with interpretation sometimes being the difference between life and death. Now she had been observed cavorting with an Englishwoman. Then she learned that Ray was a detective. "A DETECTIVE... A FOOKING DETECTIVE... OH FOOK... FOOK THEY'RE GOING TO KILL ME... FOOKIN JAYSUS I'M DEAD... I'M FOOKING DEAD!" And lastly it was revealed to her that the quiet man with the shiny scalp and glasses was a priest. "OH FOOKING JAYSUS... A FOOKIN PRIEST TOO... AND A DETECTIVE AND A FOOKIN ENGLISHWOMAN... I'M DEAD. I'M FOOKIN DEAD... THEY'RE GOING TO KILL ME... OH FOOK. FOOK!" The girl's courage and toughness had melted away.

Now remember when Fr. Pat heard profanity or sexual language, he would say, "The presence of God. Presence of Jesus!" The terrified girl and outraged priest both lost control, filling the crowded vehicle with their lamentations. Each "FOOKIN JESUS"... was immediately followed by an equally as ardent "PRESENCE OF GOD. PRESENCE OF JESUS!" The rest of us sat there amid this ping ponging of oaths wondering what the fuck was going on. The girl was rocking in her seat. The mortified priest red faced, as each of them stared eternity and damnation in the face, and we merely looked at each other.

Joanie had to talk the girl down off that metaphorical ledge and assure her that Pat was not your average Irish priest, all penance and sexual repression. Ray was way out of his official jurisdiction, so his badge meant nothing here and that she hated war, all militaries, and especially the English forces, this seemed to calm her down considerably, but she refused to exit the car for the next step we had scheduled. She was absolutely convinced that if anyone saw her in our car with its odd collection of passengers and out of country license plates, she would be killed.

Through back-channel connections between the Producers back in New York and the military here in Belfast, we had been given permission to record an interview with the local commander in the military facility. This was no Fort Apache kind of thing. Just an industrial style compound with no easily recognizable purpose in an area of similar structures. Albeit these block walls were topped with concertina razor wire spooled along their top. We approached the large metal gates leading into the compound. Here we were met by an officer who had been expecting us. I began recording immediately. The military's only rule was that I was not to record too much of the interior of the fortress or its layout. If the wrong eyes were to see what the interior looked like, it might facilitate an attack. We had not until this moment had any real contact with the Brits or local authorities. After speaking with Joan, reassured by her East End accent, the thin cigars she smoked and inspecting Ray's detective shield, the officer ordered the gates to be opened.

We were all very nervous. Our Irish go-between who had wisely chosen to remain in the car had spooked us with her hysterics and outright fear. We had already seen the troops patrolling the residential streets expecting an ambush. Nerves were frayed all around. The heavy gates crept open, and I followed. A young soldier in full battle gear was standing directly in front of me, holding an automatic rifle at the ready, not aimed but held close to his bullet proof vest. Through the protective mesh of his helmet, I could see his face, his bad complexion, eyes darting nervously right and left. I couldn't blame him for being jumpy. I had the lens of my shoulder-mounted camera staring directly into his face. I apologized for having the camera so close to him. "It's OK Mate, it's your business, right?" But his eyes never stopped watching everything around us with a mix of anticipation and dread.

Parked nearby, idling, and ready for a hurried departure, was a row of Armored Personnel Carriers undoubtedly fully gassed and loaded with weapons. One well-placed RPG would have turned the compound into a fireball and taken out much of the surrounding neighborhood. Every second that the gates remained open was a second of unnecessary risk for all within.

I shot everything that looked interesting but non-compromising... soldiers busy with chores and similar B-Roll material. We interviewed the officer, who responded with expected boilerplate phrases and reassurances that their military presence there was strictly to protect local citizens, etc.

We had exhausted our brief time within the fort. The thick, reinforced steel doors slammed shut behind us. The street was empty... the picture of serenity.... Joanie was pretty upset. She really hated war and its practitioners. She knew the twit of an officer was just blowing us off and had cooperated with us only because he had been ordered to do so. She kept referring to him as a "Toff" and "wanker."

We thanked our young Irish friend, tipped her generously and dropped her off in a different neighborhood. After leaving the car she hurried away, stopping to look over her shoulder to make certain she was not being followed and vanished down an alley... shades of Liam O'Flaherty. We were all thrilled to be heading back south. We laughed and talked about what we had seen and done. Father Pat seemed especially relieved and never had to resort to his protective mantra of "Presence of God Presence of Jesus" once during the roughly two-hour trip. Joan was driving again because we still needed to pass through border guard posts. Her accent was like gold here in the North, not so helpful in the South, however.

Taking a last pull on one of her cigars, she threw it out the window, where it quickly returned via the rear window and ran for the shelter of Ray's crotch. He began to yell as we all shifted around to accommodate his frantic movement while Joanie turned to look. These antics caused the wagon to veer left and right in a way sure to guarantee a ticket anyplace in the States and attract the suspicions of even a school crossing guard or mall cop. The guard post and road barrier were just ahead of us. Joan rolled the wagon to a stop next to the uniformed guard who asked for and examined our passports. Ray flashed his badge once again. Personally, I thought we were screwed. Our wagon had been swerving all over the road in full sight of these guys. We could not afford to be detained or we would miss our return flight. There were those large, black tubes and boxes in our back, just begging to be searched. To my delight and sincere surprise, our papers returned, we were thanked, and wished a good night.

At the airport, John and I re-labeled all of the equipment boxes, matched them to the Carnet and once we were through customs, we were nearly home free. Having now walked on the streets of both of my ancestral islands, I had resolved the long running family dispute, to my satisfaction at least. Sicily and Ireland each had a culture of resistance and rebellion. Each had managed to keep unique cultural differences alive despite the efforts of their respective occupiers to destroy them. Each had produced outstanding literary figures: playwrights, poets, and novelists whose works of art, born in these isolated locations, had been adopted by the world.

Both islands had rugged, intimidating coastlines, a maritime heritage, and shared in the individualism and resourcefulness of those adrift at sea, island dwellers. While certainly not the same, nor were they that impossibly different.

I was cold and overtired. All that we had seen, experienced, and recorded added depth to our individual lives and understanding. The suspicion, scenes of military occupation, poverty, and lack of hope had weighed on each of us. Nevertheless, we remained voyeurs, participating yet able to leave, ultimately influencing, and changing nothing. I never saw Ray or Father Pat again after our little trip as our paths diverged. I did hear that Pat left the priesthood and married. Talk about a trip!

I was ready for a change of climate and culture. Just how far was Sicily from Ireland I wondered.

DID YOU SEE FELLINI?

THE MONTE CARLO SHOW

"**B**onjour Mesdames et Messieurs, Bienvenu en France," the pilot announced from the cockpit. We were nearly there. Those 3 years of D-averages in French Class had not been a total waste of time after all. The European coastline stretched ahead of us and the ocean grew more blue with each descending moment. We had finished our flaky croissants, strong coffee, bitter Brazilian orange juice, and tabs of beurre... but not the butter Americans are used to. The French butters have much more buttermilk and are made to European standards. Take note of that designation: EUROPEAN STANDARDS. Butter would never be the same to me. Nor would ham, fruits, melons, bread, or cheese. (You get the message.) But those wonderful differences still awaited me as the plane banked above Nice Airport and gently bounced to a perfect landing. My first visit to Europe, et quel bonheur, the "MONTE CARLO SHOW" was paying. A shuttle was awaiting me, or rather us. It had never dawned on me that other people on the show crew might have shared the flight out of JFK. Not that it mattered because no one else knew me anyway. It was roughly a thirty-minute drive along the scenic highway from Nice to Monte Carlo in the Principality of Monaco. Monaco was a speck of a country but fiercely independent and just as proud. Our minibus dropped us at our various hotels. I knew very little about Monaco and only a bit more about this glamorous town. Monte Carlo had been a multi-generational hangout for European royalty, the wealthy and privileged from all points north and south. The Hotel de Paris was a Belle Epoque masterpiece and had its own ornate casino. This gaming establishment made the operators of Vegas, Atlantic City, and Biloxi look like amateur hustlers and their casinos monuments to cheap taste and neon. The Europeans had long ago learned how to tastefully separate gamblers from their money. As the Bel Hop led me through the lobby, I was truly impressed but not overwhelmed. Then he used a thick brass key to open the ornate door to my room, stepped aside and waved me through. Mon Dieu! The space was huge. I had never experienced elegance until that moment. The smartly uniformed man swung open two louvered doors to reveal my balcony, which overlooked the harbor and Royal Palace. The view was all blue sea and shattered light. The sea breeze warmth flowed into the rooms, causing the lacy curtains to billow. The room smelled like inherited wealth and lavender. Had my French been up to the task I would have said, "There must be some mistake. Did you misread the room list? Is there a Holiday Inn room still unassigned?" It would be a pain in the ass for me to unpack, lay out my stuff and then have a front desk junior manager rush in and have to sheepishly apologize and inform me that, "MON DIEU... Excusez-moi monsieur mais une erreur a ete commise." A slight mistake had been made and MY room was down the street on "Le Avenue de Howard Johnson." To my intense happiness that never happened. It was all mine until we had to leave town for Le Grande Prix when rooms like this would command outrageous prices. They became so valuable that we were paid to "leave town." My temporary destination was the UK to visit with family, but not for another month. One of the other cameramen approached me in the hotel lobby. His nickname was "Doc" and his Texas accent would probably have drawn stares even in the States. We had been invited to join Marty Pasetta, the show's American Producer, for dinner at a nearby cafe. The meal was over 4000 francs... roughly $1000 US. Doc and I only had dessert. Gulp! We returned separately to the hotel. It was a wonderful night to just stroll and savor the oleander, roses, and mimosa bushes. It took a while to familiarize myself with the primarily French and Italian being spoken nearly exclusively. Some of what I heard was intelligible to me, but this was Northern Italian, Milanese, and Florentine-Italian and not the hodge-podge of Southern Sicilian and Neapolitan curses, oaths, and vulgarities we grew up with in the States. Monte Carlo was not a "pizza by the slice" kind of town. We would be working at the Sports Club of Monte Carlo. It was a relatively short walk from the hotel. Although shuttle service was provided for the crew, several of the Hollywood guys chose to make the walk. I had been stopped for walking by the police in Los Angeles. Albeit it was Beverly Hills but still, this exercise was viewed with real suspicion by LA's gendarmes. NO ONE walks anywhere in Los Angeles. It was easy to tell the tourists and homeless from the locals because they are, you guessed it, walking. Los Angelenos drive literally everywhere, they would drive to their cars if they could. So, I was even more surprised to see so many of the camera crew strolling to the venue. Of the seven or eight camera operators, five were from Hollywood. It was only when someone told me that the walkway cut through the topless beach that the sudden urge to exercise by the LA crew made immediate sense to me. The show was a variety program intended to interest audiences on both sides of the Atlantic. American performers such as Liberace, Cher, The Oakridge Boys, Telly Savalas, Andy Williams, and other stateside A-List acts would headline each hour-long show. The rest of each show would feature popular European singers such as Charles Aznavour, Petula Clark, circus, comedy, and dance acts. Since we were so close to France there were obligatory appearances by mimes. The all-male "drag" Les Ballets Trocadero de Monte Carlo was one act that proved to me that the lucrative American Market was not prepared to embrace our show. Even stars from the United Kingdom often had little luck "crossing the pond" with their music. Humor also could be very tricky to sell to the United States. One of our acts was a man dressed like a clown hugging himself while dancing and-appearing to make out with someone unseen. It brought the house down here but would take some time to crack the ice in Kansas and Tuscaloosa. I thoroughly enjoyed working with the many wonderful performers whether they were Greek singers, Bulgarian jugglers, or Hungarian dancers. In general, our European audience seemed to both enjoy and appreciate the show more than Americans probably would. Our host was the very handsome Patrick Wayne, son of the "Duke" himself. Patrick was assisted by a bi-lingual but mostly French speaking feathered boa caterpillar named "Plume." If "Plume" were to somehow end up at a garage sale table anywhere in the United States, his canary yellow body would still be there long after the FREE sign and card table had been stolen. I never heard Patrick comment on his unusual side kick whom the French at least seemed to enjoy. Each time Patrick did the intro to the next act, the Director would stage him at a different table in the audience. Looking "tres chic" in his tuxedo and surrounded by beautiful women in gowns and bling, they probably needed armed guards to get him safely back to his room in order to honor his marriage vows. If he wasn't married, then I congratulate him on his stamina. The show also had "Les Girls," your basic Parisian and Vegas kick line of chorus girl dancers whom the West Coast guys knew from working together in Hollywood on stateside versions of variety shows. When not working, the girls and LA camera guys fraternized. Get-togethers that did not include Doc or I for the simple reason that Hollywood camera guys tended to be cliquish. Even though I was a "name" in NYC very few professionals on the West Coast had ever worked with me. My social life had been far from robust back home. It had been my hope that my prospects would improve here in Europe. That had not happened. Despite being in this most romantic location and single, I always went back to my room alone. It began to depress me. I was able to socialize with the females on the crew at lunch and dinner. A particular girl began responding to my stares and flirtations. Each time we passed we exchanged smiles. We began searching each other out but it did not progress beyond that. On my breaks I would wander back and watch her work. Sometimes she would catch me, smile, and wave.

ATTABOY

While walking late one night I happened to pass a thick hedge behind which a child had set up what seemed to be a stage. A single overhead light shone down on the piece of wood on which the child had set up plastic figures of men, women, and children in opposing groups, a classic theatrical staging. Whatever the child's intentions had been, the tableau made me smile and appreciate where I was working, what I did for a living, and how very generous fate had been to me.

My camera position was on the High and Wide shot at the back of the house. A position generally reserved for newbies whom the Director had no great faith in yet or for veteran cam ops who could be counted on but whose reflexes might have slowed. I was a newbie then and now I'm a veteran, often still working for the same Producers forty years on and off on the High and Wide. At least I'm still getting calls for shows and have around 16 Emmy Award nominations to my credit. My camera was placed on a scaffold platform set back in the darkness of the concert hall. Each time I went up or down I had to use a tall ladder attached to the back of the platform. About two weeks into our show's run, on an afternoon when we were in the middle of a slow-going rehearsal of some jugglers, my platform began to shake, someone was climbing the ladder. When I turned to see who my visitor was, a mass of curly blonde hair slowly rose above the edge of the platform floor. There was the face of the girl I had been so shamelessly flirting with but had never spoken to. We had been exchanging smoldering stares and goofy smiles daily. Now here she was. Her true-blue eyes locked onto mine. She was smiling. When she spoke, it was with a London accent. I had assumed she was French. "Will you make me a promise that before you leave Monaco... you will make love to me?" My shock was complete. My additional surprise was that she wasn't laughing. This didn't seem to be a prank designed to get a laugh at the expense of the gullible American camera guy. "Yes, of course," I promised. As far as I was concerned, the sooner the better and leaned over to kiss her. I was thinking, "How do you feel about sex atop a crude, dirty plywood plank, because it's OK with me!"

The platform rattled and shook again as her hair vanished from my sight. Suddenly things looked a lot more positive. Another character had walked onto my personal stage and life had become more interesting. It was difficult for me to concentrate on the Bulgarian guys with their balls and bikes. The girl was married of course and this being France, kind of, if you walked a little bit north anyhow, the French were nonchalant about that kind of stuff or so I had heard. Maybe all was not lost. My personal morality was that of a wandering dog so there would be no complications there. Later that week she stopped me in the theater and asked me if I was "Enjoying my time in Monaco." "Truthfully, I've only been able to travel locally," was my reply. She suggested we take a trip the next day.

She arrived at my hotel the next morning in her aged, military gray-green Citroen and we headed north, into Provence. There was a popular saying at that time that God felt guilty because he had made Provence so beautiful, He/She decided to compensate by filling it with the French. Southern France was like nowhere that I had ever been, a place so incredibly beautiful and magical. The rich history, storybook villages and sensuality of sights, aromas and floral scents appealed to me immediately. As the girl talked and laughed, I would divert my eyes away from the alluring scenery to stare at her, the blonde curls tossed by the warm breeze coming through the open windows, the cinnamon and allspice scent from her exotic cigarettes, the wonderful warmth when she would reach over to touch my hand. She told me about her life growing up in a hardscrabble working-class neighborhood in London's East End, playing in the ruins remaining from WW 2's blitz bombing. She had sex with a visiting American actor who turned out to be Errol Flynn, Hollywood's most notorious pederast. She wanted to write and perform her own songs. We would only have a limited time together that day. Our destination was a storied restaurant auberge, La Columbe d'Or, in the 14th century hillside village of Saint Paul de Vence. An amazingly picturesque enclave of small buildings, cobblestone lanes, fountains and breathtaking views of hills and vineyards. The American author James Baldwin spent the final 17 years of his life there. The restaurant had been established in 1920 and the quality of the cooking combined with its location in this scenic place drew the rich and famous for many decades. Picasso, Jacques Prevert, Yves Montand, and numerous other celebrities had been guests. Struggling soon-to-be world-famous artists like Matisse, Braque, Leger, Alexander Calder, and others often stayed above the restaurant in one of the 3 bedrooms. They paid for their bills with painted canvases which today were worth millions of dollars. Not a bad tip! During World War II, refugees from Paris and occupied France found a temporary haven here. I couldn't imagine what it must have felt like to flee for your life and all life has to offer while surrounded by the beauty of this heavenly place. To constantly fear capture, dreading the harsh thump of jackboots on the aged cobbles, having to sheepishly leave your table because some German wanted it, it reminded me of the fate of the Jews of Corfu whom the Nazi's yanked from that sun blessed island, threw into cattle cars, and shipped to death camps through the bitterly cold Polish winter.

The same family had operated this restaurant for many decades. We arrived just past lunch. The stone walled dining room had perhaps 20 tables in total. Only one other couple was already seated. Windows overlooked a verdant landscape that had been cared for and occupied for many centuries. I felt sure that among the stone walls and terraces below our restaurant there were ancient ruins, groves of fragrant orange trees, silver-leaved olives, and carefully tended grape vines. I was confident the olive oil used in our meal and the vin Ordinaire that we were sipping had come from nearby farms.

Although the meals served to us at our luxurious hotel were invariably delicious, I was pretty sure our present chef would consider us worthy of something special. I was correct. We stared only at each other, ignoring the fortune in artistic wealth adorning the walls around us.

Can you explain to me what causes that rush of excitement and longing at the sight of one specific person? The immediate thrill of their presence? The strong desire to be with them and only them? That sudden surge of emotion that causes steady hands to shake, blunts the appetite and leaves you distracted during the day and sleepless at night. I thought of only this girl. She was the missing piece to the puzzle I didn't know I was trying to solve. She took my hand in hers and placed it on her cheek. She was trembling. If it made any difference to the owners that only one of us was wearing a wedding ring, they didn't let on. Would it have mattered which partner was being unfaithful? I was guessing that the male would get a pass but probably not the female.

The bread served to us was crusty and flavorful. Just imagine, bread with an actual taste. We each dipped small pieces of it in the brightly colored ceramic dish of oil provided. We had salad nicoise, she gave me her olives. If a room can be said to surround you with care and serenity, this was it. The probably long deceased owners had created not just an auberge, a restaurant, but an actual experience, richly textured and appealing to every human sense, of sensuality itself. I had been gently, willingly seduced by a girl, a place and a moment in time. Her hand lay upon mine on the starched linen tablecloth. Afternoon light glowed in her hair. She encouraged me to try escargot for the first time. I let each buttery smooth, garlicky pearl roll around on my tongue. The meal of veal chops, spring potatoes, and young asparagus was life changing although with our nervousness, our appetites were limited. We each had a Cream Brulé and after thanking our gracious waiter, began to stroll through the lovely old town.

Nearly forty years later, my wife and our two children would return to this same restaurant. Several decades in the life of a man mean nothing when compared to the life span of a centuries-old village. In my heart remained images of the girl, the serenity and peacefulness of that long ago afternoon. Was the girl still married, even still alive? I would never know.

The chef had stepped outside to grab a smoke and some fresh air before the dinner rush. Hoping the fates might be smiling on me, I described to the man that long ago lunch, how important it was to me and was it at all possible that he could squeeze us in for another memorable meal and experience for my family. He looked at me with kind amusement and told me, regrettably, that they were booked for lunch and dinner for the next four months.

After thanking him for his sincere inability to accommodate us, we set off to tour the tourist packed town. What could I have expected after nearly forty years? Has tourism increased that much? Americans and a more peaceable generation of Germans seemed to be everywhere in the village, alternately buying and sighing.

On that long-vanished afternoon, the girl and I drove back to Monte Carlo as the sun was sliding west, radiant with peach and crimson hued light. Once back in my room, I lay on the large bed, left the balcony doors open to the moonlight and replayed in my mind the day's images, repeatedly, until I slept. We were limited to seeing each other at work. My mind was preoccupied with her despite the show's many entertaining performers and distractions.

Doc and the Hollywood guys did their thing and I attempted to fill my extra time. Day trips by train to Italy helped. On my return from an overnight trip to Venice our train was stopped near the border. The gendarmes removed EVERY person of color from the train, luggage and all. No exceptions and no information given. This was twenty years before 9/11. I was trying to get back to Monte Carlo in time to show up for our afternoon call time. Leaning out of the window of one of the passenger cars I watched the parade of bewildered, nervous, and understandably frightened passengers pass my car. Some dressed like vendors, others in native dress and quite a few business types in suits and sports jackets. People pulled luggage, others carried bundles or large bags. "I'm screwed," I thought. By the time they interview all of these people it will be amazing if I'm there by show time. It was my turn now to be anxious and confused. Then just like that, the train pulled out of the station leaving well over 100 people stranded in a strange city with probably no idea why they were being retained or for how long. Had this been the United States the civil suits would still be working their litigious way through courts. Things were certainly done differently in Europe.

Each of our shows had an American headliner combined with relatively well-known European performers often totally unknown in our country. American stars like Dionne Warwick, Melissa Manchester, and Kris Kristofferson were certainly recognizable in Europe and some like David Soul, were bigger stars in the UK or France than they were back home. Even the most unusual of the acts was entertaining. French singers were especially popular with the ladies. My beautiful friend worked backstage with the artists, and I continued to pump out my high and wide shots. At last, my friend and I had an opportunity to be alone together after she fabricated an excuse to be out late. She arrived at my hotel room door and gave a soft knock. In minutes we were in my king-sized bed together. Before we could begin to make love, the bedside phone rang. A man with a heavy French accent asked me if the girl was there. Covering the receiver, I asked her who knew she was in my room, like an American idiot. A Frenchman would have guessed the identity of the caller, the purpose of the call and simply said, "Non monsieur, c'est impossible" and hung up. "It's my husband," she said and held out her hand for the phone. Her skin was so warm, one of her feet was stroking my leg. They began a feverish conversation in vitriolic French, a language that even when shouted and yelled still sounds incredibly romantic. "I must go my love," she said as she dressed. Feeling gallant and guilty, I offered to go down to the lobby with her. "No," she cautioned. "When I go down, he will have to slap me around to protect his honor, but he won't hit me hard. If you're with me though it could get serious. There will be other Frenchmen witnessing what happens." She saw the look on my face, kissed me, and said, "Don't worry, I'll be fine." Then she was gone. I got back into the still warm bed, lay on her side of it and imagined the worst that an insulted Gallic honor could do. The next morning found me in my usual seat on the crew shuttle. We were waiting for the driver who stood nearby, smoking like a film noir bad guy. Suddenly Doc turned to me and said, "Hey, did some French guy call your room last night wanting to speak with the show's 'Lead' cameraman and demanding to know if his wife was in bed with him? I told him we didn't have a lead cameraman but he insisted!" Christ, I thought, I'm screwed. Since my presence on the crew had barely been acknowledged by the others it would be interesting to see how the very proud, very competitive Hollywood camera guys would react to the news that one of us had been claiming to be the show's most vital camera person. The storm was not long in coming as the other operators boarded. Each of them had received a similar phone call. It soon became apparent that it was "Mr. High and Wide" who was the offending crew guy. They were more amused than annoyed. Thankfully they did not know who the wayward spouse was, and I stayed mum. A show is like a small town, news, insults, and grudges spread quickly.

Once at the venue, she hurried by me while managing to grab my fingers in passing, smiling as she did so, one bright blue eye ringed with a shiner. At least it wasn't the nasty kind of handiwork that one sees some wife beaters capable of. It turned out that her Algerian girlfriend had known about the intended liaison, told her husband who was a buddy of the girl's husband, et voila! The Algerian girl didn't know my last name only that I was the "Lead Cameraman," so the husband had called each of our rooms! Merde certainly, but it could have been murder! We were both lucky. My promise to her would need to wait.

The weeks and performances quickly passed, and we had arrived at our last day in Monaco. A traveling circus was drawn up outside the 'tres chic' Sporting Club. Several filthy cages from one of the "IA" countries: Bulgaria, Romania, and Slovenia, held several mangy brown bears. Since it was known that even humans were often neglected there it was no surprise that these animals looked so pathetic. There was no PETA in the former Eastern Bloc nations. The bear's fur was discolored and stained. These guys would never end up as rugs, they were too far gone and made their fireside cousins look positively energetic, even when splayed flat and with their insides long gone. Tufts of their originally brown fur had been bitten, clawed, or yanked out of their hides. They lay around in a torpor, the tongue of the largest hanging over his lip. How was it possible that this much stench could accumulate in an unenclosed space? Their handlers made the average American carnival worker look like Goldman-Sachs management trainees! To the untrained eye it was even possible that the wrong set of mammals was caged. When it finally came time to rehearse them, the animals were led onstage. Out in the main part of the theater, waiters were busy setting up the tables for that night. The expensively dressed patrons would claim their highly prized tables in just a few hours. Since this was our final performance, Princess Grace herself would be attending again along with her dashing husband and their gorgeous children. Official Royal Family photos resembled Ralph Lauren ads. Nothing lights a fire under the asses of the English and Europeans like the presence of Royalty. The beautiful American actress Grace Kelly had bloomed under royal care and had become even more lustrous and alluring. She was born to be regal, pampered, and honored. According to every gossip source, she was a great Princess, well loved and respected within their tiny realm. I had been introduced to her playboy son Prince Albert. No, not the one that peculiar bodily mutilation is named after. This one was charming, handsome, wealthy, and royal. Check please! He had befriended one of our production assistants who himself did not realize he aspired to the royal lifestyle until he had met and hung out with Albert. The pleasures of royal life hit him hard. Good old Los Angeles, Knotts Berry Farm and the Galleria would never satisfy him now. Back on stage the bears began racing around on bicycles, each wearing a tiny pillbox hat. I'm sure bears do this routinely in the wild, right? The biggest wise ass on the Hollywood crew said over headsets that he personally didn't get what was so special about bears riding bikes, he did it all the time! As we were laughing and getting shots of the animals on their bikes, the biggest bear leapt off his tricycle and bolted for freedom. It was now or never. His large brown body flew off the stage, flattened a few tables and ran hell bent towards the kitchen. For once it was lucky for me that my high and wide camera had been placed on a scaffold platform. There was little chance that Ursa Major would find his way to me. Utter chaos erupted in the large dining room. Waiters began screaming, not merely yelling; these were shrieks of pure terror. They were all immigrants from somewhere like Bangladesh, waif thin and short. The bear had bet the house on this escape and any of the waiters standing between him and freedom was in for a forced day off. We could follow the frantic animal's progress through the corridors and alleys of the kitchen area by the screams, crash of plate covered trays, and metallic cascades of silverware. The screams became less frequent but more shrill as the waiters and kitchen staff fled through back exits. I imagined the poor bear was just as frightened as the staff. Gendarmes with guns drawn arrived and followed the fugitive bear, who was soon cornered and caught alive, thankfully. No one was hurt and there was a lot of joking among the service staff afterward about them needing to change their "French briefs!" After all the excitement, the Director broke us for dinner. The Girl and I sat at different tables, each with our respective departments. I would catch her looking over at me, gifting me with a radiant smile while laughing along with her co-workers. In truth I knew no reason why she had chosen me nor what her side of the attraction was. Surely, she was as aware as I was that any possible relationship would be brief at best. As far as I was concerned, she had been sent by those gods and guides who watch over and minister to our sorry asses. Perhaps we both simply desired the energizing intimacy no matter how fleeting or temporary the connection. She made me feel alive and that was good enough for me. After the trainer and gendarmes had done their "Wild Kingdom" thing, we returned to the theater.

Bomb sniffing dogs were led through the venue and some very serious looking paramilitary and Legionnaire types had joined with the plain clothes security detail. As soon as the theater was filled with the audience, the royal family made their entrance. The crowd stood, applauded, and cheered. Lithe necks craned for a better view. The curious rose on tiptoes and shifted shoulders as they tried to get a glance of the Royals. Even I felt chills of excitement at this Camelot moment with a rolled Rrrrr French accent. It isn't every day that an American gets to be around Royalty. We needed to settle for the rentable by the hour politicians that govern us, colorless liars, thieves, and scoundrels as they invariably turn out to be. We began the show. I think the American Country band Alabama was the night's American name draw. Country music is surprisingly popular in Europe and the United Kingdom. Germany has several Wild West parks which feature gun fights, rodeos and entertainment that ole Wild Bill himself would have enjoyed and approved of.

Our crane camera operator, Hank Geving, a bearded and quite handsome member of the Hollywood crew, drew many appreciative stares. His position on the crane made him even more conspicuous. He had inadvertently caught the attention of a corpulent man wearing a cape and wide brimmed hat. Hank hadn't noticed so his camera assistant clued him in excitedly. "He is the great Italian Director Fellini. He is sitting very near us and I'm thinking he likes you. He has been staring." Hank glanced casually at the rotund man surrounded by admirers. It simply wasn't his thing and working regularly in Hollywood, this was merely another "so what" celebrity moment. Federico would have to scout for talent elsewhere tonight. The long lens on my camera allowed me to at least look at the man but as he was seated with his back to me there was little to admire. The show moved along to the Circus act and the hatted bears were ushered onstage where they obediently ran to their waiting bicycles and began pedaling furiously. The larger bear was not among them. Perhaps the other bears were thinking, "Shit man, we TOLD him not to do it!" My hope was that the bear was just being forced to sit this one out and lucky for him. Had he attempted his escape while the Royal Family was seated in the audience, he would have been dead before his scabrous body hit the floor. As the show progressed toward its grand finale, the dome covering the entire theater slid open to reveal the Mediterranean night sky. Fireworks flared and arced across the starry expanse while the audience applauded, cheered, and my super wide lens caught it all. It was absolutely thrilling. A bona fide Cinderella moment for yours truly as what could compare with this? In a week I would be back home living in my version of a pumpkin and heading into New York being pulled by New Jersey Transit white mice. Following the show, the Producers had rented out the super trendy and always crowded nightclub JIMMY Z'S for our official Wrap Party. Crew and production people wandered in as they finished their last tasks. The girl was dancing with other crew members, local workers, and anyone who asked her while keeping an eye on me throughout each dance. She looked relaxed and joyous. As after most television productions, these parties celebrating the completion of a show are also melancholy events as most of us may never see each other again. There would be intense hugs, tears, and futile vows to remain in touch. We stayed long enough to hear the speeches from the Director and Producers, then we snuck away from observant American, French, and especially Algerian eyes. The serious drinking had already begun and our absences would not be observed. Cupid would be especially busy as alcohol loosened inhibitions and sex would become a universal language transcending French, Italian, and English. The venue we had been working in was situated on a promontory overlooking the Mediterranean Ocean. We could sense and smell it rolling toward us unseen and somewhere below the cliff edge.

We stripped and made love in the darkness, crushing the soft grasses beneath us. The breeze was cool on our sweated bodies. Aware of what might have been and could have been after our desires were satisfied, we lay on our arms beneath the blanketing darkness savoring these moments of aloneness, together. Then she sprang up and standing nude in front of the large brightly lit fountain, threw her thin arms wide with happiness just as it surged to life, silhouetting her nakedness against its blazing light and cascading water, the blonde curls tumbling down her spine as our last moments together faded like the fireworks had, and our lives began their inevitable drift apart.

MY BEAUTIFUL
CHILDREN
THE EMMY
AWARDS

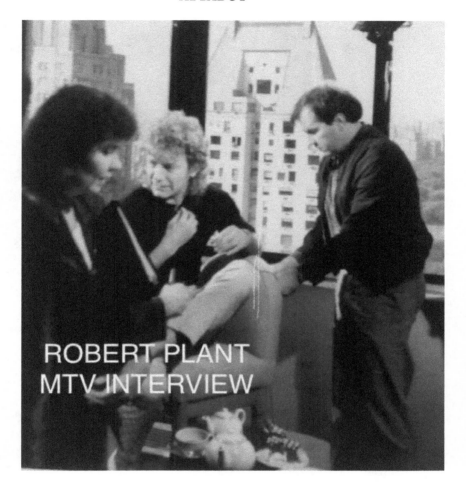

RECORDING ON THE STREETS OF BELFAST - WE WERE FREEZING!

HALF STATUE OF CHRIST IN IRELAND

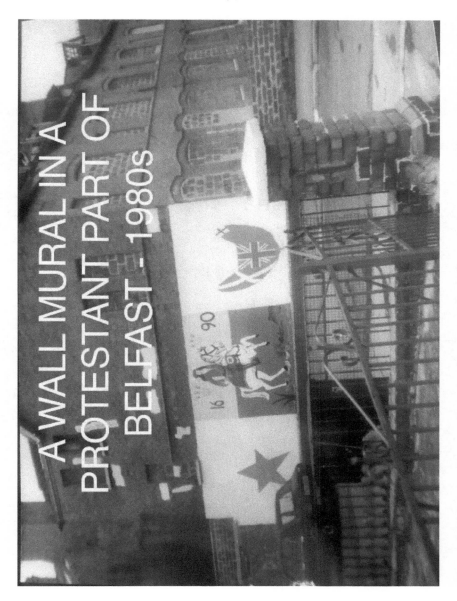

A WALL MURAL IN A PROTESTANT PART OF BELFAST - 1980s

FORMER NEIGHBORHOOD IN CATHOLIC AREA OF BELFAST 1980s

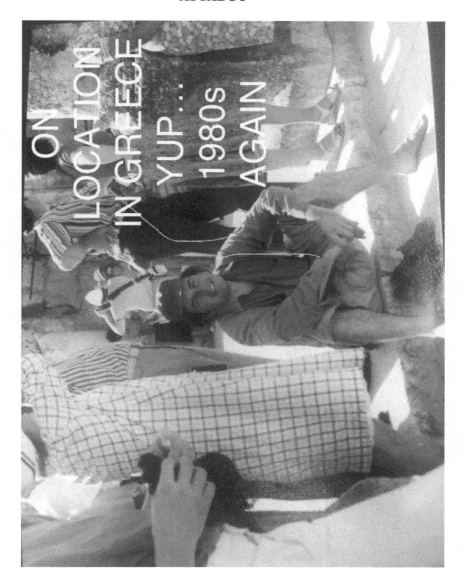

MTV SPRING BREAK
DAYTONA BEACH
1980s

A QUIET MOMENT BEFORE LIVE FROM LINCOLN CENTER BROADCAST

MY TWO FAVORITE BEARS THE BIG BLUE HOUSE 1990s

LADY GAGA

It was Mother Monster herself who instructed our Director, the good natured Alex Coletti, to deliver a message to me, "Tell him that if I see him eating a donut, I'm going to take it out of his fucking hand and shove it down his fucking throat myself!" Having delivered this threat according to Lady Gaga's instructions, Alex shrugged his shoulders and smiled as if to say, "I'm only the messenger." "Were you eating a donut," he asked me. I told him no, that as much as I like sweets, donuts never appealed to me. Neither one of us knew what Mother had seen but I had been forewarned. Being blessed out personally by Lady Gaga herself, was certainly a way to start a show!

I knew now that I would be shooting her while she was watching me. I'm an average middle-aged guy with a gut. Maybe Gaga just assumed that as a union guy, donuts were my preferred food source. The camera ops would certainly be easy to spot scattered as we were amid Mother's Little Monsters, who were already streaming into the repurposed warehouse on the grounds of the sprawling, historic Brooklyn Navy Yard, spread along the shoreline of Manhattan's East River. Although it was early evening, the river was busy with barge traffic, excursion tour boats, a few pleasure craft, and Coast Guard patrols. Manhattan's east side was an array of skyscrapers aglow with millions of brightly lit windows.

One of the old naval warehouses had been turned into an art gallery and concert venue. Gaga had chosen this location for the dropping of her new album partially because Brooklyn was rapidly becoming New York's "Left Bank," gentrifying rapidly. Artisan coffee places, craft beer distilleries, art galleries, and other trendy businesses were crowding out the older merchants in this heavily Hasidic community. There had been some confrontations over the unwanted changes. The notoriously conservative and insular Hasidic viewed these changes as a threat, which of course they were. These new arrivals represented multi racial and cultural values as well as lifestyles that were anathema to their rigid religious orthodoxy and straitjacket conformism.

The entire donut situation was making me nervous. Unfortunately for me, my camera assignment had me directly in Gaga's line of sight, on a scaffold above a soon to be wall to wall mass of Mother's Little Monsters. My job was to follow her around the large stage keeping her in a full figure, head to toe shot. It's hard to screw up an assignment like that unless you become bored, get distracted and look away. What transpires then is one of a camera operator's worst mistakes, looking at an empty viewfinder because whomever you were supposed to be following intently, has walked out of your shot when you looked away. The Director's screaming commentary will help you to concentrate again. "CAMERA THREE... WHERE THE FUCK IS SHE? WHAT THE FUCK CAMERA THREE... WAKE THE FUCK UP!" This is most definitely NOT, an Attaboy!

Although we were here to celebrate the release of her latest album, "ARTPOP," we rehearsed songs her fans already knew by heart and were expecting to hear, including: "BORN THIS WAY," "HOPE," and other previous releases. A particular favorite of mine was "APPLAUSE," which was on "ARTPOP." If you have never watched any of Gaga's music videos, begin with "APPLAUSE." Either it will make you want to dance or sell everything and move to the country. Which country? Who gives a shit, the world is ending anyhow.

The piece is a visual assault, extremely well directed and with edits sharp enough to cut your corneas. A much-heralded part of this event was Gaga's "Flying Dress." Critics still referenced her iconic "Meat Dress" and that loathsome garment's debut was long, long ago on the popular culture timeline. A new gimmick was needed. We were not sure what to expect. Was she going to fly around the venue? There was no overhead arrangement of wires that we could see or were aware of. Jetpack? Crazy and probably illegal in an enclosed space. When the moment arrived to demonstrate the flying dress, it worked, but merely floated her straight up into the air and then back down. Fans expecting Gaga to soar above her assembled faithful would be disappointed. With this devoted crowd, it did not matter because she could do no wrong.

The former warehouse was filling rapidly. We had our catered dinner. Guess what was served? Can you guess? No? OK... MORE trays of dry crusty lasagna, desiccated chicken parts so brutally hacked one could easily believe that Jack the Ripper was now a Brooklyn based caterer, a white kind of fish, which fish? A species of fish with what appeared to be legs, if that helps!

I was just in the middle of finishing a piece of cake when Alex, the Director, approached me again. He looked concerned. It was I that should have been concerned.

"OK, this is NOT my idea. Gaga wants you and Evans to put on one of her jumpsuits. Remember, I'm just the messenger!" If I had not already eaten the cake you could have shoved it neatly into my open mouth. A fucking JUMPSUIT? These monogrammed, white garments were designed for much, MUCH younger men and women, one size and sex fits all. Anyone over 110 pounds could not possibly fit into one. Evans looked at me; he's both shorter and considerably heavier than me. WTF?

Together we walked to Gaga's wardrobe department. When I told the women what we were there for, they both laughed. I mean seriously LAUGHED. When they noticed that Evans and I were still standing there, one of them said, "OK... wait a minute, you're not fucking kidding, you're serious?" "Serious as a heart attack," was my answer. With an understandable roll of the eyes and long experience with Gaga and her wishes, they pointed to a rack of identical white bodysuits and said,

"Pick one, they're all the same."

Carrying our trendy new duds that might help me pass for a vibrantly hip but very confused 50-year-old at best, we headed for our cameras. By this time everyone else on the crew knew that the two of us would be wearing skin tight jumpsuits. Stretching them over our bodies could make you weep for fabric. Both of us knew that camera phones would be at the ready expecting to document our humiliation for eternity or on FB, whichever lasts longer. I was determined no one would see me dressed in that until the very last second.

It was getting difficult to make my way through the teeming crowd who circled slowly around the large hall. Our camera platforms were islands of middle aged, overweight, straight guys surrounded by a sea of androgynous and openly gay men. There wasn't a single natural woman to be seen. Black and white films of Gaga walking nude through fields and woods were playing on television sets hung from around the walls but no one seemed to be watching them. There was a large bronze statue of Gaga on display. She was sitting nude, on her ass, and her legs were spread wide open. It could have been a memorial to a particularly famous gynecologist! Groups of her fans were stopping for selfies in front of it and I was certain many of them had never seen what it represented in the flesh, at any time in their young lives. I didn't think they regretted not having had that experience either.

The event had the festive excitement of an adults-only Halloween party. Mother's Little Monsters were an imaginative and creative bunch. There were numerous wildly inventive "looks." One man was wearing a wooden birdcage around his head. Periodically, he would open its little door with its twig thin bars and bring a cigarette to his lips, take a covert drag, and then close the door as though to imprison the smoke. I'm sure if the door were left open, then it would ruin that most important "impression."

Evans messaged that he was unable to get his jumpsuit above his knees. My intention was to wait until the very last minute to change. I realized it would be a good idea for me to pee before the show. Not a second too soon either, as there was a long line stretched from within the men's room into the theater. I joined it at the back. A young man turned and after gracing me with a warm and friendly smile said, "Oh Honey, if you have to actually use the toilet, don't wait in line, these bitches are just checking their makeup!" After thanking my thoughtful young friend and seeing two burly stagehands just walk right by the line, I followed them. He had been so correct. Other than the stagehands, no one was using either the urinals or stalls. The full-length wall mirror hanging above the sinks however were 4 or more males deep jostling for an unimpeded view in its reflection.

Near the back of my platform was a stack of large, black metal cases on wheels, used for carrying sound equipment. Hidden right in the center of them was a space into which my body fit and where my jumpsuit was yanked and wiggled onto my body, over my underwear. Although it was as secluded and private a place as was available in that very crowded room, it was not private enough. Turning to my right, there was a young man watching me through a separation between the cases. His face expressed nothing, neither interest, amusement, nor a hint of embarrassment at being caught peeping. Another smoker, he lifted the cigarette to his lips, inhaled, and allowed the smoke to drift away, watching me as though I was an unusual specimen in an aquarium tank. The jumpsuit had made it over my gut and buttoned up to my neck. The first deep breath might be enough to fire its buttons like bullets!

After the climb up the platform to my camera, the stairs were removed. Although I usually have a few snacks handy for me to nosh on during other shows, that would not be the case tonight. God forbid "Mother Monster" should see my mouth chewing. Besides, my jumpsuit had no pockets. When I glanced down at the crowd below me, a fashionably thin, well dressed young man stared up at me, his tongue flicking in the air like a snake searching for possibilities. Best to keep my eyes glued to my viewfinder.

The show was being delayed due to a technical issue, it was some of her equipment, not ours. House music filled the venue and despite its volume and beat, no one was dancing. A roundabout stream of Little Monsters flowed in a dense crowd around the entire room, checking and being checked out, like schooling fish in a huge tank. The buttons on my play suit burst open. They had done a heroic job.

I thought it was wonderful that so many people who might otherwise have a difficult time fitting into conventional society due to temperament, sexual preference, or for other reasons could find happiness and inclusion here, being themselves and finding acceptance under Mother's musical mantle. She was the Pied Piper of real diversity.

When the concert began for real, Mother was generous to her Monsters. She rocked the multi-level stage with selfless energy, the crowd was ecstatic, and shouted their love and appreciation at her. Like most concerts, the time raced by. She never once left my camera frame and for the long drive back home afterwards, I stopped at a Dunkin and grabbed a coconut donut. No one paid me the slightest attention.

THOSE SOUNDS OF SILENCE

I was in a no-work, no-girlfriend funk, so it seemed like a good idea at the time. The ad in the Tampa Bay Times promoted things you could do if you were bored or literally so lacking in imagination that you needed them to make suggestions to you, or words to that effect. Anyhow, the ad was for a celebration of the SIMON AND GARFUNKEL CONCERT IN CENTRAL PARK. That show, taped in 1981, was a widely anticipated reunion of the two former best friends and musical hit makers from the 1960's and 1970s. By the time of the reunion, the audience had more genuine affection for either performer than they had for each other.

I had not seen the show since working on it 45 years earlier. That is not unusual for me as most of the 3500 or so shows that had my name in their credits had never been seen by me since they were recorded. Not an intentional avoidance, just basic indifference on my part. Spending time with my family, reading, gardening, and train travel were my preferred time killers.

What had excited me now was the opportunity to see the show on a theater sized screen and not the home TV set, no matter how many inches wide it was. Only a tiny number of the shows I worked on ever made it to theatrical distribution and even then, they were usually being broadcast live, so guess who couldn't go because he was working!

Being an optimist, I had bought two tickets figuring a companion would materialize. It was an average size theater, the screen a little smaller than expected but what the hell, this was going to be great. Placing my jacket on the vacant seat beside me, surprise, no companion had emerged, I settled in to watch the show. I had not paid much attention to the band setup placed in front of the screen. On the evening of the reunion, Simon and Garfunkel also had a backing band. The show was a sellout. This was my first shock. Not the popularity of the event itself but the nature of the audience who had arrived to share this big moment with me. The audience was nearly all elderly. A parade of walkers, canes, and portable oxygen containers came through the theater doors. Some people even seemed unaware of where they were. They looked worried and even concerned as in, "Where's the dinner Marge," confusion.

I comforted myself thinking these people probably attended every event here. It would not have mattered if it was a BEE GEES cover band or a revival of KISS ME KATE. Maybe they were season ticket holders. The distraction did not work for long though. Minus the infirmaries, we were peers. The realization of, "Don't kid yourself buddy, you're that old too," seized me.

About the same time, I understood that this was to be a tribute concert and not a film showing, I might as well have scalped a couple of pricey tickets to see the Beatles and gotten Beatlemania. An announcer came on stage and thanked the crowd for coming, then plugged upcoming acts. Following that commercial and the ever popular, "With no further ado," out came the musicians. The audience showered the stage with applause, waking more than one of the attendees for sure. Out came the drummer, guitarist, and bass player, who were welcomed with polite clapping. Then the Simon and Garfunkel impersonators themselves, who received enthusiastic applause. The men were WAY too happy and effusive. The actual performers had been thrilled at the welcome that greeted them that night in 1981 but were surprised and intimidated by the size of the crowd. They had not performed together for 11 years. The duo had begun as your basic 1960's folk act playing clubs and theaters. No promoter would have considered them an arena draw, yet here they were about to entertain half a million fans.

The impersonators performed the same show repeatedly, on a touring circuit of small-town stages and dinner theaters. The show today was likely to be more parody than honorarium. The Paul Simon of the duo began by reminding the house that the crowd who had attended the original show was the 7th largest for any American concert, 300,000 attendees were expected to fill the Great Lawn in Central Park, according to New York City police and the Parks Department. His figure was incorrect. Nearly 500,000 people eventually congregated in that fabled place, a crowd size comparable to the Woodstock Festival, which was nearly the largest crowd for any music event in our nation's history.

When he asked the crowd if anyone there had been in the mass of fans, a few people clapped. That gave me an odd sense of kinship with at least a few of these walking wounded and their companions. My hands remained in my lap, however. They began the concert in show order, beginning with "Mrs. ROBINSON." One singer stood at the microphone at the front of the stage while his partner sat at a piano. They wore big, happy grins and did everything but invite the crowd to join them on stage in a kumbaya hand clapping sing along. I was certain that the flood of wonderful memories would bring tears to many of the attendees. Judging by the advanced age of many of them, a few wet seats also. They were cute and cheerful. As performers, they were probably sincere in their admiration for the original artists. It was not that they put on a bad show or butchered the music; the concept itself was what annoyed me. It reminded me of a LIFETIME ACHIEVEMENT AWARD at the Oscars or the entertainment on an oldies cruise. It was time and memories preserved in formaldehyde.

When the projected images of wildflowers and hippie style crowds began to appear on the screen behind them, I arose from my seat and left the theater, easing the door closed behind me. A trio of older docents, volunteer ushers, were standing in the lobby talking together. When I came out of the theater, they looked concerned. One of them asked me if everything was ok. Was there a problem with my seat? Thanking them for their concern and admitting that I had expected something different, the kind woman then said, "Oh dear, did you think it was going to be Simon and Garfunkel themselves?" They all looked at me as though I had made my escape from "the home" and was non compos mentis, which is a polite way of saying a bit "loony." After explaining to them what my disappointment was about and revealing to them that I had been at the concert and was one of the cameramen, they looked at me curiously. Not exactly looks of admiration, but of puzzlement and then suspicion. This same reaction has bothered me in the past. One night while sitting in a bar, a woman gave me an appraising look and said, "So what do you do?" She was eyeing the book I was reading. "You a teacher or something?" I explained to her that I was a television camera operator at the ABC Network in New York. Sizing me up once again she practically sneered, "You're full of shit. You don't LOOK like a goddamn cameraman!" End of the interrogation. It did not seem as if these gentle women accepted that possibility either. Just another wannabe pretending to be me!

By 1981, Simon and Garfunkel had not performed together in 11 years and were estranged. Artistically and personally, they had become vastly different people. The concert in the park would be more than a reunion between two talented artists. They would be performing in the heart of their hometown not far from Greenwich Village where they had first appeared in the 1960s. They knew firsthand how critical a New York audience can be.

The concert had attracted a lot of media fanfare and every camera operator in New York was hoping to get a call to work on it. Michael Lindsay Hogg had been hired to Direct the show. Michael had received critical acclaim for the recent English television production of "BRIDESHEAD REVISITED" which he Directed in addition to the Beatles concert film "LET IT BE" and numerous high-profile productions, including the Rolling Stones. He was as heavy a hitter as hitters can be.

Although I was relatively well known among camera operators in New York City, my expectations of landing a spot on the event were not high. The weeks passed. Then the call came in, adding my name to the crew. I had previously worked with English Directors such as Lindsay Anderson, Brian Large, Bruce Gowers and Sheldon Larry. They were very reserved and creative, polar opposites of their American peers. English Directors were used to cooperating with camera operators who had worked their way up through the English studio system and the BBC. They were invariably polite and appreciative of our suggestions, which were accepted with professional respect, even if they were not always followed. If any of us screwed up a shot during taping, the Director's response was likely to be a deep sigh and screaming silence or perhaps a reprimand such as "Oh that's too bad camera five... I was really hoping you could get that shot!" Devastating to hear, enough to move even a non-drinker like myself to try and drown away the self-loathing. We really wanted to perform at our best for the English, they were well respected professionals that none of us wanted to disappoint.

In later decades with the increased tapings of rock and roll concerts, American crews would get to work with Directors from the UK who were just as abusive and as inclined to scream as the worst of our home-grown lot. American Directors, with rare exceptions, were generally more blunt in their criticism. "WHAT THE FUCK HAPPENED THERE CAMERA FIVE... WHERE WERE YOU DURING REHEARSAL... I'M NOT SURE THAT I CAN EDIT AROUND THAT FUCK UP... JESUS CHRIST. YA REALLY FUCKED ME THERE FIVE!!!!"

Michael was slightly built, fashionably thin and hiply dressed, and I mean LONDON hip. He was wearing the kind of expensive leather jacket that might send an impressionable camera operator directly to Barneys after rehearsal to price and buy a similar jacket before doing a WTF reappraisal of the item in question and realizing that a director can afford to spend a few days wages on an article of clothing, but not necessarily a cameraman, especially one likely to leave it hanging in some restaurant after he left. Michael asked us many questions about our camera placement, equipment and invited us to offer suggestions. It was a great feeling when a director openly treated you with respect and professional courtesy. He was used to working with the best camera operators in the UK and Europe. In NYC, we were his team and he expected us to be very good at what we did. Our talents and opinions were respected and none of us doubted our value or importance to this production. We were there to carry out his vision and that is all we wanted to do.

My camera was on stage and my primary responsibility would be Art Garfunkel and a two-shot relationship between the two performers. It was mounted on a rolling pedestal, the wheels of which would enable me to move around both men and frame shots of them relating to the audience. The crowd began to gather during our sound check. The lawn seating was already tightly packed. The concert would not be until the next night! Nevertheless, we knew that many fans would remain overnight, camping out to reserve those precious spaces closest to the performers.

I was standing at the lip of the stage which was quite high above the audience. Spread out in front of our platform was a Woodstock Redux vista of multicolored blankets, folding chairs and people sitting, talking, and laughing together. Heads resting on partners shoulders, hand holding, some meditating and others reading... a panorama of peace.

Garfunkel walked up and stood beside me, hands in his back pockets, a stance he favors. He was very surprised at the size of the crown already gathered near the stage. "We're scared shitless," he confided. This was my first hint of the performance anxiety suffered by so many artists. The gut pinch and churn of not doing well and disappointing the fans. It's called "flop sweat" by the pros and is a reason why comedians insist on keeping the AC cranked to a frigid high, so the crowd won't see that sheen of anxiety begin to coat their upper lip and brow.

"Some of these people have been here since yesterday," I told him. "You guys OWN this town. They're all here for you!" He smiled and thanked me then walked back across the wide stage. I was not just trying to make him feel better, I meant every word of it. Oddly enough, when I shot the "ROBIN WILLIAMS ON BROADWAY" special for HBO, my camera was backstage, next to Robin. Before exiting through the wings to walk on stage, he gave me a gentle smile and said, "I'm scared shitless man!" It's understandable why a performer would grab that last sip of scotch, final puff on the joint or turn to whatever other substance they might use to cure the jitters, before making that walk into the searing light and longed for applause.

On show day, the huge crowd filled every square foot of the Great Lawn, an area where sheep once grazed a hundred years ago. Following our catered dinner, we took our positions and the show began, with "Mrs. Robinson." The heartfelt enthusiasm, cheering and applause never stopped. How any performer could look into that crowd, feel the powerful energy washing over them and not realize how sincerely this city loved them, did not seem possible. Both men must have felt so special and blessed.

I worked my pedestal and lens for all they were worth, adding my little bit to the montage that would commemorate this event, so proud to be a part of the show. I shared in the happiness of the audience as the wonderful songs were sung live, less than 20 feet away from me. Unlike some musical acts whose work I was unknown to me, I knew each of the songs being performed. Every song they sang brought with it a rush of personal meanings and experience. Memories of former lovers, far away cities, wonderful hours spent with friends, and hours spent alone. A lifetime of emotions and images were encoded within the notes of Paul's guitar and the sweet harmony of their voices.

Sometimes, I would turn my camera towards the audience to get those humanizing cut-away shots of people singing along, kids riding on their parent's shoulders while others danced, fingers and hands signing WE LOVE YOU!! It was amazing to think I was being paid to be here. The show photographer Susan Gray took a photo of me on camera, framed and gifted it to me a month later.

An overzealous fan managed to somehow scale the high wall beneath the stage and ran past me towards Paul and Art. He was quickly removed by security but it crossed my mind that maybe I might have stopped him, although he was well past me by the time he caught my attention, as my eyes were concentrating on my viewfinder. These kinds of things were still treated with amused, slight concern then. The apartment building where John Lennon would be killed soon after, was visible from our stage and after Reagan's assassination attempt, security became extreme. There was just too much nutty chasing too little celebrity.

The audience was hushed for ballads like "THE SOUNDS OF SILENCE," loud and celebratory for the more up-tempo songs. I was loving every beautiful second of it. The duo had appeared to slip easily into their former roles. There were gentle smiles of mutual appreciation, reminders of their former relationship before the rancor and mutual recriminations. Tonight, they were not solo artists with the distractions and pressures of alternate career paths. Tonight, they were the charming and self-effacing guys that had helped a country to forget about racial riots, an Asian war, and murdered leaders. Tonight, they were the duo we all remembered, celebrating their city, loving and being loved in return. Tonight at least for two hours, they were SIMON AND GARFUNKEL once again.

WALLENDA IN CHICAGO

It was the highest rated show in the Discovery Channel's history. Twenty-million viewers tuned in to watch Nik Wallenda possibly plummet into the Grand Canyon. The ratings were even better than those of their perennial boffo SHARK WEEK, for a single night anyhow. While still in Arizona during our stay there for his Grand Canyon crossing special, I overheard him at breakfast with his family, discussing the possibility of doing his next walk across Midtown Manhattan. The idea made me smile. Property owners, insurance underwriters, and city officials might be a more formidable challenge than passive natural obstacles like Niagara Falls or even the Grand Canyon. My guess was that with the legal obstacles alone it would have been easier for Nik to receive permission to pave the Grand Canyon and drive over it than to cordon off Midtown Manhattan. Good luck with that dream my fearless friend.

Because of the strong ratings for the Arizona program, I was not surprised when NBC called me to work on the next Wallenda project. It was another joint production between NBC and the Discovery Channel. Ron de Moraes would be directing once again. Eve Adair had also returned as his Assistant Director. This time the 454-foot walk would be between three buildings in downtown Chicago, one of them the Sears Tower, nearly 700 feet above the Chicago River, in November, which is already winter in the Windy City. Of course, why not. Not content with one walk between two tall buildings, there would be two separate walks and for the second one, Nik would be blindfolded, and the path would be up an incline. If he had any real balls, he would grease his 2-inch-wide wire and hire snipers to take pot shots at him... gutless.

Of course, I readily accepted the gig. I had begun to realize that so long as Wallenda's death wish drew viewers there would be ever bigger and wilder walks to come. In mid-November, I flew northward from sunny Florida. I was wondering if anyone at either of the decidedly secular media empires had asked Nik to dial back the religious talk. Probably no one had because the shows were a ratings success, and no one would consign Nik's piety to the broadcast dustbin until the ratings or the daredevil himself fell. Perhaps he did have a direct spiritual hotline to God the Father and Jesus who were "sponsoring" him for reasons known only to the Divinity. God works in strange ways but maybe he keeps an all-seeing eye on the Nielsen Ratings.

We could not forget the participation of Megachurch Religious Personality Mr. Joel Osteen. A man willing to take time away from his money-making multimedia empire to deliver his prayer invocation attempting to add a religious dimension to these walks, treading an even thinner ethical line than Wallenda's wire. Wouldn't risking death to a God given life for such a frivolous reason as show ratings qualify as questionable by Christian ethics? Someone should ask Joel when he gets out of his private plane.

Our first day on location I walked from our hotel to our staging area. The various camera assignments were made. Cameras were scattered all over the downtown area surrounding a busy bridge that crossed the Chicago River. This time my assignment was not at Home Base (DRAT!!) but on a "game camera," shooting Nik. That notorious lake effect wind was running rampant along the wide streets. The city told the production that no one was being allowed on the rooftops selected for our use because of 65 mph gusts. I was back to dealing with the capricious winds that had so tormented us atop the rim of the Grand Canyon.

My camera was on the roof of a 39-story hotel. The distant building was pointed out to me. It would be a bracing walk. Standing in the blowing snow while my eyes counted the floors of the hotel to its summit, the icy wind reminded me of what to expect once I reached the building's roof. As somebody joked, "Look at it this way, when it begins to snow, you'll be the first to know!" We lost much of the morning's rehearsal time waiting out the wind. Following lunch, the weather had improved enough for us to venture onto the roofs.

A lobby elevator carried me to the 38th floor. Here I was met by a gruff and impatient uniformed man. He impressed me as a busy guy from the building maintenance crew who already had too much work to do and did not need the additional bullshit of having to give me a tour of the roof. Together we walked up a narrow staircase to the penthouse. This was a strictly off-limits area. Huge machines operated in the noisy gloom. Each one controlled one of the elevators that ferried hotel guests throughout the building. I was led to a low wall of sliding windows and followed the man through the opening, stepping carefully out onto a narrow, gravel covered ledge. In front of us was a crevice-like gap separating our hotel from another building across a side street. The man had me put on a safety vest which had a long, red nylon rope attached to its back and sternly warned me that this vest would need to be worn anytime I was out here. We walked out onto the wide roof and its unobstructed view of the Sears Tower, Chicago River and the area to be covered by the walk.

Now there was an additional warning, "You have enough line to get to your camera, perhaps a little further. If you fall, the line will stop you just past the top floor. You will be hanging there. Once I leave, no one will be coming up to check on you, so be careful. Good luck buddy." A burst of blowing snow swirled past me as he left. The nylon safety harness tugged at my back and lay like an umbilical cord, attached to the steel structure of the roof. The cold wind nudged me as I walked carefully to my camera, and sat on the ice-cold metal case that would serve as my seat. I placed the ice cold headsets over my ears and steeled myself for the coming six hours of work that still lay ahead.

My view of midtown Chicago was impressive. Skyscrapers surrounded our hotel. I was congratulating myself for the foresight to bring and wear my heavy-duty parka, two fleece lined pullovers, a sweater, wool cap, and two pairs of socks. Like a Michelin Man, I was ungainly, with restricted movements, not that it mattered, where could I go but over the side, right?

Ron was thoughtful enough to give the camera operators numerous five-minute breaks. Time enough to pee, if we were near a toilet, or to grab a quick snack, or warm up with a cup of tea. Unfortunately for me there was nowhere for me to get to in that amount of time. My fives were spent in the room with the noisy machinery. I was completely alone, peeing into a coffee cup left on a table long ago. The giant machines were constantly shutting on and off, whirring and creaking as the lubricated steel cables spooled in and out and the elevator cars carried passengers somewhere below our floor. A single bulb that lit the dirty, industrial room was the only illumination. After warming up, it was time for me to retrace my path through the open window, reattach the harness and walk carefully along the parapet, back to my camera. I hugged the wall of the building, keeping one hand against its reassuring solidity. I am not a fan of high heights.

By this time the smears of standing water which had previously pooled amid the roof's gravel had frozen over, gleaming, and hazardous. Just what I did not need. Walking would be dicey. As a test, I gave my lifeline a solid yank, it held. I keyed in on my headsets periodically to remind people I was there and listening. If no one had heard from me in a while and God forbid some accident had befallen me, someone might notice my absence. It was worth a shot.

It was rush hour now. The bridge was packed with cars and throngs of pedestrians heading home. Lights in the office and residential towers around my immediate neighborhood began to snap on. I watched as workers left their offices for the night and saw the cleaning crews moving through the fluorescent lighted rooms, dusting and mopping away the day's business. The sun was gone, withdrawing what pathetic comfort it had offered during the afternoon. The wind became stronger, making me shiver despite my layers of clothing. I could feel the chill creeping down my spine like a spilling liquid.

The most difficult part of my job was the incessant cold and isolation. A few papers littering the roof near me were snatched up by the wind, swirled in wild eddies and then sucked over the roof's side. Ron, the Director, had many juicy, sexy shots to choose from. Unlike the canyon, all of the cameras would be able to feed him exciting shots. The camera in the helicopter would have a particularly stunning view. Making noisy passes high above the circus of searchlights and mass of spectators that were expected to attend, despite the cold. Chicago's residents are a hardy bunch. The show promised to be every second as exciting as the Grand Canyon walk had been, almost guaranteeing a follow-up somewhere remote and dangerous.

The roof ended roughly 18 inches to my left. I could literally reach my left leg out and touch space. I had little to do and was concerned that I might doze off in the gripping, relentless cold, which could prove fatal.

Several times I stood up to stamp my feet and flail my arms in an attempt to generate some muscle warmth and restart my circulation. After rehearsal wrapped, I hurried back to the hotel, had a good dinner, hot bath and cranked the room heat until all traces of the day's chill left my body.

That next morning we were very pleased to discover the weather was forecast to be milder, although still windy. The city had requested residents living around the event area not play loud music from their terraces during the actual walk as it might distract Nik. They were still welcome to sit on their terraces, belt back the hamburger sliders with a few cold beers and watch Wallenda taunt death. Despite pleas from the show's producers that no one shoot lasers at Nik's face and eyes, we already knew that some would and they did. Anything for a thrill or cheap laugh, right? What could a tiny green concentrated beam of light do to hurt a grown man? Blind him? Another woke infringement on their right to participate in the event. We rehearsed until dinner, another hamburger consumed alone by me in the lobby level sports bar surrounded by the din of game commentary and audience cheers. I was happy to return to my dismal den and made my way back to the machinery room, which was warmed solely by the heat from the machines themselves. The expansive and otherwise dingy space reeked of lubricant and looked even more forlorn and isolated than it had yesterday. The large drums throbbed and hummed, ceaselessly spooling and unspooling the elevator cables. Sudden, loud clicks as each elevator was summoned, still startled me.

It was time to get to my camera. Exiting through the window, I stepped onto the parapet. Next to me was the darker chasm separating my building from its neighbor. The space was not as wide as that in front of my camera but it felt more menacing, like the bottomless cleft in a glacier. I avoided looking down, pulled the heavy safety vest and attached harness awkwardly over my shoulders and belted it against my chest. With my left hand sliding along the cold aluminum panels of the windows to keep my balance, I crossed the still icy, windswept and relatively dark parapet corridor and out onto the open roof. My camera and metal carrying case looked pathetically puny in the darkness, both stationed at the far corner of the roof and back lit by the mass of light rising from street and river level.

An estimated 65,000 people were crammed together along the riverbank esplanade and were kept in place by barriers. A mulling, moving mass generating a surge of noise which was very audible even up here. Our show helicopters made grumbling passes through the night sky. Ron loved the aerial shots with their drama of packed crowds, mass of lights and spiraling motion.

The long length of the lifeline pulled on my harness and back. With 65 MPH wind gusts still a possibility, this was no time to take chances. Its squiggly red length looked like a magic marker gash on a sheet of white paper. I was comforted knowing that it was securely attached to steel girders and that the camera tripod had been bolted to the roof. After taking my seat behind the camera I waited for the fun to begin. Because of the extra-long lens on the camera, I was able to look at the viewers on their terraces and down at the crowd. Groups of excited people were killing time laughing and fooling around with each other while practicing their whoops and cheers. Most were wearing sports related swag with logos for hometown teams like the Cubs and Blackhawks. Their laughter and shouts escaped in breaths that froze on contact with the frigid air.

I reminded myself that as per the instructions given at our camera meeting, if Nik fell this time, we were to follow him to the ghastly conclusion, an impact that would invariably become a video viral sensation. The producers and networks would cut away to a neutral image or that age old standby TROUBLE SLIDE just to cover their asses with the FCC. Not a great idea to have the children at home or impressionable adults see the actual splat. I imagined kids breaking away from playing their video game long enough to glance at the tragedy unfolding on the TV and mumble, "Cool!"

As revealed earlier in this story, heights unnerve me. While still in college and driving through upstate Pennsylvania, my car needed a quick fix. Leaving it with a garage and setting off to do a little exploring of the rural village, an abandoned railroad trestle was revealed beneath a dense grove of sumac, linden and various kinds of trash trees and saplings. Tentatively testing the remaining strength of the bridge's beams, I began to walk out along the rusted girders high above the abandoned tracks. I was alone, knew no one and no one knew where I was. If only Common Sense was a course option in every college curriculum! About 20 feet beyond solid ground, I simply froze. The fear was instant; my legs began to buckle, sweat drenched my skin. Locked in place and trying to suppress the wobbles, my only option was to get hold of my fear and try to control it. When my body calmed down sufficiently, I slowly turned around and with one shaking foot in front of the other and outstretched arms for balance, I inched my way back to safety. Wallenda could have his heroism and heights.

Since then, I have sometimes wondered why I took that chance. I certainly was not a kid, realized the chances of getting hurt and had no peers to taunt or jeer me into doing such a foolish thing. So, the question remained, "Why?" What inner compulsion or weakness led me to do something so obviously stupid to even the somewhat mature adult I considered myself to be? Why do we dare ourselves or anyone else?

Why would Nik challenge gravity and elemental natural forces like the wind, the limitations of stretched steel strands or the torque and twist of a thin metal line? Is it just about beating the odds, even if it's yourself doing the odds stacking? At least with deep oceanic exploring and journeys into space or lunar landings, there is a benefit, if sometimes minimal, to humanity. With self-indulgent pastimes like sky diving and high wire walking, no one benefits, except the Networks and perhaps Joel Osteen. What remains is just the thrill of rolling the dice and betting your life. When do we stop proving ourselves to ourselves and to those we think actually give a shit?

From my rooftop corner, the crowd roar surged skyward, carried by the cold wind. Artificial light radiating from the lighting instruments placed around the audience and river area. I contrasted the very different experiences between any one person standing within that mass of people and myself. They were surrounded and probably somewhat warmed by the proximity of so many others. They would strain their neck staring straight up at the rooftop from which Nik would appear and patiently watch him begin his walk, their cheers or yells submerged within those of the many thousands.

I would be able to follow each of his steps along the vibrating 2-inch steel wire, monitoring his facial expressions and hear his nonstop supplication of God the Father and Jesus, praising their power, flattering their Divine attributes and begging them to protect him, from himself. Here I was, perched at the 90-degree angle of two roof lines with only the minimal light from surrounding buildings to help me see, totally alone. Struggling to keep my shivering arms and hands from shaking my camera shot, the heavy nylon cord weighing on my spine. My lens extended beyond the lip of the roof. When zoomed widest it gave me the optical sensation of being beyond the roof itself, suspended in space, well beyond safety.

When Nik finally stepped onto the wire, a roar welled up from the crowd. I'm sure he savored the sound and took some of his physical and psychological strength from it. He took his initial, hesitant steps onto the wire, judging the mood of its steel heart, his feet feeling for its strength and reassurance. Helicopters from other media outlets hovered noisily above, unable to come lower due to restrictions and mandated distances.

Nik began his litany of prayers. A miniature camera had been attached to his chest, its view was straight down, past his balance pole, beyond the well-trained feet in their soft looking slippers and revealed the wide vacancy spreading nearly 800 feet below. The shot was bottomed with bright light and the shifting, screaming crowd, whose cheers and yells rose up to meet him, audible even through the headset he wore to communicate with his father, whose job was to monitor the conditions of the air and wire.

In Arizona the virtually daylight walk showed viewers just how immense the canyon space was... the majesty and high walls of unforgiving stone... the distant gleam and trickle of the Little Colorado River. Here in Chicago, there were far more distractions for him to contend with. Towering windowed walls looming above and stretching below him. Each building glowing with light, spectators and noise.

I fed Ron whatever shots looked interesting from my location. Much of the time I was free to punch up the other cameras on my viewfinder and admire their work and how Ron blended the shots to create the rhythm of the show and convey the excitement we all felt. Nik was solid, confident, and secure in his skills. Raised a showman in a show business family, he knew how to provide the viewers with exactly the entertainment and thrills they wanted. He did not disappoint.

The show was another exciting spectacle, fast paced and exciting. Nik completed the first of the two walks, which drew an enormous cheer from the thousands of fans watching from below. He then tied the blindfold on for the second leg of the walk. This would be up a 19-degree incline. Taking a few exploratory steps, searching in the self-imposed darkness for that all important steel wire, he made contact and began the final walk. This was finished more quickly and its completion and his success were rewarded with more sincere, full throated cheers and whistles.

Wallenda had once again beaten gravity and managed to ignore the distractions of the enthusiastic crowd, the noise from helicopters constantly shifting around him, lake effect winds, and many thousands of eye-catching lights. He had triumphed once again. I felt sure that this show would prove another ratings bonanza for the Networks. Undoubtedly, they would return to Nik at some time in the very near future and ask, "What have you got for us? What's next Nik?" Only Wallenda knew that.

TORO

I arrived in Mexico with a bad case of Philadelphia Airport Food Court Revenge! I had to keep leaving the long line at passport control to relieve my distress, then return to the back of the line to await my turn again. After managing to buy a bottle of Pepto Bismol and swallow a few slugs of the chalky pink brew, it began work to its magic on my intestinal tract. I then located my name on a cardboard sign and let the driver hurry me safely to my hotel.

The Producers had wanted me to take a cab from the airport, but I patiently explained to them that I did not speak Spanish and was quite concerned that my cab might end up whisking me to some cartel hideaway and then demand a high ransom. There had been several such kidnappings. Since the Production was already resisting covering my airport parking fee, I reasonably deduced that a six-figure ransom demand might meet with their disapproval.

To avoid being in an unmarked grave in some Sonoran Desert, I insisted on being picked up. Eventually most of the other crew people did the same. Gringos! By the time the car left me at the hotel, I was exhausted. The previous evening's shoot had gone much later than scheduled. The flight had been bumpy. Oh, bed where art thou?

The nap was refreshing, the sight of my black tongue in the mirror was not. WTF? It was typhus black, bubonic plague black, not the pink fleshy, wiggly appendage I was used to seeing housed behind my teeth but a morbid glob of char. "What fresh hell was this," to quote Dorothy Parker. Was a plain old kidnapping still an option? Maybe the grave would have a nice view of mountains! I had not eaten or consumed a liquid since landing except for the Pepto; so much for being cautious and careful. I figured I needed to contact the hotel doctor, assuming they had one somewhere. Thankfully, my search crossed paths with the show's Production Manager who explained to me that the local Pepto turns tongues black. He didn't know why, it just did. Not to worry.

Following dinner alone in the hotel restaurant I stopped at the lobby bar where the rest of the crew was. The hotel bar is where every show in any town, anywhere in the world would hang out... the de-facto meeting place for crew calls, business gossip and reunions. A place to "press the flesh" and let everyone know that I had arrived safely. A couple of the guys grabbed quick glances at my tongue and probably resolved not to share any drink or bit of food with me.

Early the next morning, the three of us on the show's set up crew arrived at the local stadium and began to load cameras and other equipment onto metal carts. The metal boxes were heavy and awkward. We had piles of bulky camera cables, tripods, and other stuff necessary to set up and broadcast a live television show to somewhere else. It's what we call "hump" work as it involves the back more than the brain... real "tote that barge, lift that bale" stuff.

We were all expecting a day of skinned knuckles, pinched fingers, and metal parts falling onto sneaker clad feet. A brutish "push this into that" exercise, laying out a ganglion of electric cables, and expensive equipment that would eventually result in viewers who subscribed to HBO being able to enjoy a boxing match Live from scenic Mexico.

The three of us began pushing the overloaded and non-motorized carts up ramps and into the arena. A group of young Mexican guys watched Todd, Luis, and I muscle and coax the loads with genuine surprise and amusement. Perhaps they had never seen gringos doing the grunt work they were used to doing... pushing and tugging like mules. Each of us was already sweat drenched and dirty, our clothing grease grimed, and faces dripping with perspiration in the humid air. They were probably thinking, "Madre de Dias. HBO flew these guys all the way to Mexico from North America just to haul shit around. These guys must be experts at loading, unloading, and moving shit!

We can learn something from them!" There is an art to assembling all that gear. Some of it is delicate electronic equipment but what these guys were observing could have been done by any of them, with guidance and some training. The trick is that later that day, we would need to magically morph into cameramen, artists with delicate hands, composing and feeding shots displaying great composition and interest. Then late the following night we would join the rest of the crew in disassembling and boxing that same equipment for shipment. Pulling cables along floors that were a stew of spilled beer, sticky soda, puke, and every other kind of crap that can be casually dropped to the floor, we would wrap those filthy, heavy cables into bulky coils, hoist them onto our shoulders and load them on carts and trucks which we would then roll out of the stadium and load into the large mobile production studio truck. This work would take hours to do and last well past midnight.

Our broadcast venue was a mid-size bull fighting rink with a sand covered floor and wood walls from behind which the bulls would emerge. The tiers of seats and steps were filthy with muddy boot prints. Being inside this place was like having to work at the bottom of the most stained urinal in the filthiest gas station in rural Georgia or Florida. A miasma of piss and fear fogged up from beneath the sand and confronted us head on; it lunged for your throat and nose like a starved ferret. Although there was probably blood in the sand, the prevailing note in this brew of torture and terror was vintage urea and primordial piss. You don't get used to it. The stench got worse and more pungent if it rained, which of course it did. How lucky could a bunch of guys get?

During our first day all we needed to do was run many hundreds of feet of cable, set up and test the equipment to make sure everything was working and lastly, look at shots with the Director, Marc Payton, once he arrived. HBO was the only sports producer with whom I have worked. I'm strictly an entertainment shooter with zero interest in any sport both personally and professionally. By around 4pm or so we were ready to return to the hotel, shower, eat dinner, and head to the lobby bar. This time my visit was brief and after changing in my room, I went to the outdoor hot tub and submerged there, watched the stars shining far beyond the fringe of palm trees that surrounded the tub. The days stresses and strains left my back and limbs, eased away by the hot water which penetrated to my very bones.

Since our show time was going to be quite late, and HBO would cut to our venue after 11 pm, I had the morning to myself. Sweet relief so I decided to enjoy a massage at the hotel's spa and slipped into the thick cotton robe that was provided. They even had a posh pair of monogrammed slippers for me although they were more mucho than macho. The young attendant led me to an interior room via the pool area, which hotel staff referred to as La Plaza de los Pendejos. Here I was paraded through an encampment of beautiful young, tanned bodies with my gut straining the contours of the robe, precious slippers, and black stained tongue. It was hard to ignore the stares and snickering.

Once in the little poolside massage hut, the attendant had me remove my robe and lie on my back. The air was fragrant with coconut oil, New Age music oozed from a boombox, tropical light shone on my naked body through cracks in the wood ceiling and loosely boarded walls. I was willing the aches out of my sagging, scarred torso; imagining the touch and press of the warm, experienced fingers kneading my aged body, bringing relief. Then my attention was caught by the giggles and whispers of kids' voices. Their eyes probed through the seams and gaps in the wood walls, I saw them pushing each other aside for a better view of you knew who lying you know where in the you know what! It was gringo show and tell time, even better than TV.

I had requested a female masseuse so when the masseur entered the room, he seemed annoyed and tense, even angry; he was someone more in need of a massage than prepared to give one. I brought the kiddie voyeurs to his attention. He yelled something in Spanish, directing it toward the peanut gallery. The kids scattered. After looking me over and frowning, he simply said, "Si... Si," saying yes to a question neither of us had asked but to which he now knew the answer.

He then grabbed my shoulders as though yanking me to safety from the path of an invisible automobile. Thumbs were driven into my shoulder blades as he kneaded me like a lump of dough that had somehow pissed him off. I winced with the pain. This was good for me, right? My black tongue lolled from the side of my mouth. He was working me over with the fervor of a medieval inquisitor. This was going to be a long 60 minutes. The stress began to return to my body with renewed vigor. At one point, he picked my legs up and folded them back as though he thought his missing car keys might be hiding beneath the base of my spine. This had become gringo show and tell. Like gulls, the kids had returned to their peepholes. I'm sure I heard the words "gringo taint" as the masseur pressed down on my legs as though trying to close a suitcase that was too full. This was beginning to feel like a film I caught my college roommate watching many years ago.

During the latter part of this "relaxation massage," I was ready to pay him to stop. If he relaxed me further, I would tell him my mantra, email pass code, or deepest darkest personal secrets just to stop the torture. When the solid 180 minutes of pain of the 60-minute massage was over, I hobbled back to my room to recuperate and prepare for the 10 hours of actual work that still lay ahead of me. After meeting with the crew in the lobby, we set off for the arena. At every intersection I half expected a carload of cartel type desperados to box us in and, you guessed it, hold us for ransom. OK it never happened but it does help to be at least aware of such possibilities when traveling. The arena was mucho busy. One old man carrying ice blocks gave me a nearly toothless smile. His deeply tanned face was as heavily wrinkled and craggy as the nearby hills. Frozen water dripping from the child sized chunk of ice soaked his denim shirt. There were Mayan ruins not far away and the ancient carved faces seen on its stone walls were identical to those of the men working around us. Outside the arena, generators rumbled ceaselessly, adding the reek of diesel exhaust to the potent mix of odors.

Rows of police and security guards ringed the building and congregated in knots, some with riot shields almost as tall as they were. Machine guns and shotguns were everywhere. The cops avoided eye contact. If I accidentally caught their gaze, they turned quickly away. Not exactly hostile but not your neighborhood cops either. There were local police, federales, and sinister looking SWAT teams in all black, body armor, and dark sunglasses. The varied uniforms and designs made it look like a fascist fashion show. For a boxing match, we couldn't help thinking they knew something we didn't.

We did a full rehearsal with all the crew in position. Every camera was fired and fed back images. Lights were blazing. Hundreds of feet of different kinds of electric cables were all working fine. Even the piss smell seemed to exceed itself with reek. The crew dinner was next.

Our meal was going to be catered. A sketchy kitchen produced aluminum trays of some form of food. Possibly meat but none of us wanted to bet on it. The last thing any of us needed was an upset stomach while on camera, during a live show for an important client. There would be no emergency bathroom breaks during a two-hour long show.

Best to be careful, I loaded my plate with fried bananas, salad, and several pieces of chorizo. I joined the other cam ops at their table. Chorizo is a delicious dry sausage popular in Spanish restaurants. I had just finished wolfing down my fifth piece of this spicy delicacy when one of the local guys mentioned that this was Mexican chorizo. I asked him how it differed from the Spanish kind. "It's raw," he answered casually. Raw Mexican - raw meat! My mind and stomach grappled with the concept. My tongue had just begun to return to pink again. Dear God. I ate raw, unrefrigerated meat, in Mexico, where even the water could give you the trots. Is that where the losing bulls ended up? Holy shit! I thought. "What next?" But then realized, I already knew the answer, and it was back in my room, in what remained of the Pepto bottle.

The night of the fight the arena was packed with screaming, cheering fans. Cases of local beers were consumed with pugilistic fervor. The soldiers were still visibly jumpy. The generators roared in competition with the incessant blare of the nearby road traffic. My fellow cameramen, Todd and Luis worked the ringside cameras, where they were soon splattered with blood and sweat. My assignment was a two shot of the boxers in the ring, always keeping both fighters in the shot until one of them hit the canvas and the other one jumped up on the ropes, arms raised in triumph, and I would get the "hero shot!" of the sweated, swollen face... mouth guard forcing his mouth to pucker in a grimace. Once our director received the "all clear and goodnight" from HBO, we were free to begin our "strike," breaking down everything we had so carefully set up on the previous day. The fights that had broken out between audience spectators during the Main Event had now spilled outside the arena. The heavily armed troops and police were already gone. Food and alcohol vendors had done well that night but also left rapidly. We again wondered what they knew that we were unaware of. Stagehands were already at work taking apart the temporary stage. We stacked our boxes, cases and piles of spooled cable onto carts, and wheeled everything back to the trucks. The lot would be shipped back to the states ASAP. It was after 3AM. By now, everything smelled like piss, including us. The noisy generators had been silenced. Hot and creaky, they sat behind safety fences. The lights had been removed from around the ring, which itself had returned to quiet with the stench of piss. I couldn't tell you who won the fight and didn't care. My early morning return flight to New York City would get me there just a little late for my next job, the "Rock and Roll Hall of Fame," at the Waldorf-Astoria Hotel. With luck

I might get some sleep that night. The bottle of Pepto Bismol remained within arm's reach all night though, just in case.

VERTIGO IN CHICAGO

2005

C hicago is one of my favorite cities in which to work. Top notch audiences, strong trade Unions, world renowned Art Museum, boat tours of Lake Michigan and the Chicago River, Blues Clubs, and enough other quality diversions to keep an out of towner fully occupied.

My assignment here was to work on the taping of this stop on the Irish band U2's VERTIGO TOUR. What we recorded here would be included in the DVD release. Our Director Hamish Hamilton was one of the UK's best known and busiest television Directors. I had last worked with him when we taped U2's ELEVATION TOUR DVD in Boston. Talk about an enthusiastic audience for an Irish band!

Chicago also has a lot of Irish Americans in its population, so this was also expected to be another wild event, not that you needed to be any part Irish to appreciate this band.

My first experience working with them was at the AMNESTY INTERNATIONAL CONCERT which we shot in New Jersey, in 1985. Right across the river from New York City which also had a sizable population of... you guessed it... Americans of Irish descent. Crowds in these three cities would easily rival those in Dublin, Belfast, and London.

At the Amnesty Concert the band was still finding a fan base in the United States, although it was already well known in the Boston, Chicago, and New York City triad. At that show in New Jerseys carcinogenic Meadowlands, Bono strode onstage wearing a buckskin fringe jacket, long hair tossed around in the probably toxic heavy breeze that came off nearby New York Harbor. He looked like Sean Penn's character Jeff Spicoli in "FAST TIMES AT RIDGEMONT HIGH," only a lot smarter, a whole LOT smarter! A bit cocky and commanding, savoring the wild applause the band received from the overheated crowd which had been standing all day under that fierce NJ sun. I think it was during their set that the stadium crew turned fire hoses on the crowd, showering them with cool water, to provide some relief. At least the lucky ones who were nearest to the stage benefited. I'm sure Bono approved. We all knew the fans packed so closely together in the sweltering heat must have been miserable. It also brought uncomfortable reminders of the water cannons used on Irish kids rioting in Ireland's anger filled streets during "The Troubles." Beneficial intent and milder water stream but the images were all too similar.

By 2005 Bono had become a renowned and influential World Citizen, and spokesperson for numerous humanitarian causes. He was matured and worldly, gone was the attitude and long hair. Bono and U2 were the face of progressive ideas and actions. Showing the world of entertainment that artists of all kinds had a responsibility to restoring order and mercy to a strife torn and need filled world. Along with Bob Geldof, Sean Penn and other performers they demonstrated that Celebrity has its responsibilities in addition to its privileges.

On the day of our arrival in Chicago, all of the camera ops went to the venue where the concert would be held. This gave us an opportunity to check out our cameras and make sure we were happy with their set up. It was also a chance to check out our sight lines to the stage. Knowing how the band members arrayed themselves while performing, it allowed me to assume my responsibilities would be the drummer, Larry Mullen, Adam Clayton, the bass player, and The Edge on lead guitar. It was already known that Bono did not like shots of him from my side of the stage.

U2 was undoubtedly one of the best loved and most respected of stadium band behemoths. Their tours were invariably big money makers. Each album release contained enough hit singles to keep the band fresh and guarantee radio airplay. We had a brief sound check which enabled the Director to check out our shots and determine if he was satisfied with what we could get him. We broke for a catered dinner and by the time we returned to our cameras, the indoor stadium was filled, the air thick with the sound of thousands of fans conversing, laughing, and yelling... the excitement and body heat palpable all around me. I felt like an island situated directly in the path of a river of love and excitement flowing from the upper tiers of the audience bound for the still vacant stage.

Under circumstances like this concert, we all wore special noise canceling headsets otherwise hearing Hamish would be impossible. He was an excitable Director but being English he never shouted or screamed. His instructions were always carefully worded, clear, and calmly conveyed to the cam ops who were fully caffeinated, hyped up, and ready to kick ass!

The Director on any show like this sits outside of the venue, in a tractor trailer tricked out as a mobile television studio. There are television monitors (sets) for each camera, each tape machine, one for what is actually being recorded onto the master tape, another for him to preview any shot before actually having to "take" it. It can be bewildering. To the extreme right of the Director is the switcher, which is operated by the Technical Director (TD) who actually takes whatever shot the Director chooses. In the UK that position is referred to as the Vision Mixer. To the Directors near right is the Assistant Director who keeps the Director up to date on time, tape roll-ins, etc. The Assistant Director is the Director's right hand and like the co-pilot on any flight, ready to step into the Director's chair should something happen, which it has and undoubtedly will again.

The Director picks shots from those being offered him by the 12 or more camera operators. He or she basically assembles the main show and will edit it later to correct mistakes or pick a better shot which might have been overlooked earlier. The camera operators generally always operate as if we were "live." Every shot is carefully framed, and focused. If we add a zoom or other move to the shot, it needs to have a beginning and resolution. A good Director will trust us and stay with our shots until it is obvious that it can go no farther. As soon as we have fed a shot, we immediately search for the next one, all of us competing for the Red Tally light and that all important "Attaboy!" It is a competition among peers, and that contest had begun.

Hamish began his selection process: "THAT'S FUCKING BEAUTIFUL TWO... TAKE TWO... THAT'S NICE CAMERA SIX... READY SIX... TAKE SIX... STAY WITH BONO SIX... SOMETHING ELSE CAMERA EIGHT... GOT THAT ON THREE CAMERA FOUR... GET ME EDGE... FUCKING GORGEOUS CAMERA ELEVEN... TAKE ELEVEN... GET ME THE DRUMMER'S HANDS FIVE... HOLD FIVE... TAKE FIVE... TILT UP TO HIS FACE NOW... BEAUTIFUL MATE... CAMERA ELEVEN GET ME A BONO AND EDGE TWO SHOT... TAKE ELEVEN... FOLLOW BONO TO ADAM... THAT'S GREAT ELEVEN... STAY WITH HIM ELEVEN... WIDE SHOT CAMERA TWELVE... TAKE TWELVE... SLOW TIGHTEN TO THE STAGE... JIB CAMERA GET READY TO SWEEP THE STAGE... READY JIB... TAKE THE JIB... THAT'S BEAUTIFUL JIB—NICE AND STEADY... CAMERA TWO GET ME LEAD GUITAR FINGERS... TAKE TWO... FOLLOW THE FINGERS UP TO HIS FACE... THAT'S GREAT TWO... WHAT YOU GOT ON EIGHT... OH EIGHT I FUCKING LOVE IT EIGHT... TAKE EIGHT... BEAUTIFUL SHOT EIGHT... STEADY CAM READY TO CIRCLE... BONO... OK... READY STEADYCAM... TAKE STEADY... BEAUTIFUL STEADY SHOW ME THE AUDIENCE BEYOND HIM... BRING THE DRUMMER INTO THE BACKGROUND NOW... OK STEADY... BEAUTIFUL... I'M GOING TO GET YOU OUT OF

THERE NOW... OK READY THREE... TAKE CAMERA THREE... BREAK OUT OF THERE STEADY.

This continues for two hours, maybe more if it was Springsteen or a jam band like Phish. It's a battle of our skills and experience against the chaos of a live event where musicians are constantly changing positions and the audience provides additional opportunities for shots like banners, dancing, the ever-photogenic boogieing girl on her guy's shoulders, singing faces, and even tears on occasion. Thinking on our feet is always the rule of the day.

After the concert and drop off at the hotel, we headed to the lobby bar. It was a chance to discuss the show, offer praise to those whose shots particularly impressed us, and let the adrenaline stop coursing through our veins, the knots of tension in our backs dissipate, and the shaking to stop. To savor the positive energy of a good show or nurse away the burn and pain of the bad night we all sometimes get. It only takes one bad shot or one crappy camera move to ruin your night. If the mistake is bad enough, you may never work for that Director or Producer again. There is a saying among camera ops, "You're only as good as your last zoom!" As one of the veteran camera guys, they joked about my career trajectory, when you start off it's, "Who the fuck is Jim Scurti?" Which becomes, "Get me Jim Scurti!" Then, "Get me somebody as good as Jim Scurti!" And the cycle ends with the inevitable, "Who the fuck is Jim Scurti?" At that point in my life, I was halfway along that path. I left the bar on the earlier side, around midnight.

We were scheduled for a mid-afternoon call time. There was an opportunity for a little adventure! Following a great breakfast in the hotel dining room, I took a cab to rendezvous with a river tour boat. The itinerary was a tour of the more notable Architectural Highlights along the river which meanders through the heart of downtown Chicago and the Loop. My call time for the night's show was 3PM. The tour left at noon and was roughly 90 minutes long. There was even time to grab some lunch before the shuttle to the stadium. Feeling fat and happy, I boarded the boat.

Other passengers began to arrive and pretty soon my chair at the front of the deck was surrounded. The captain announced that they were requesting all passengers to turn their cell phones off. Since my phone was my lifeline to jobs, I just silenced the ringer. The boat left the pier landing once it was completely full. I felt relaxed, ready for a little sightseeing and sun on my face. Gulls cried from above. The crowded boat began its journey through Chicago's notable Architectural history, an impressive litany of the names of famous American Architects. The sunshine sparkled upon the water, our wake burst against seawalls and the windows of the tall buildings glinted in the early afternoon light.

My phone vibrated in my pocket. It was my good friend and fellow cam op Bobby D. His voice sounded stressed and he was whispering. "Where the fuck are you," he hissed. "I'm on a boat," was my response. I was confused; why should Bobby care where I was. "WHAT THE FUCK ARE YOU DOING ON A BOAT? WHAT BOAT? WHERE DID YOU FIND A BOAT? ANYWAY, IT DOESN'T MATTER... WE'RE WAITING FOR YOU IN THE SHUTTLE! I TOLD THEM YOU WERE IN THE TOILET!"

Now it was my turn to ask questions. "Why are you already in the shuttle? Call time is 3PM." Bobby replied, "THEY CHANGED THE CALL TIME LAST NIGHT. HAMISH WANTS US IN EARLIER TO LOOK AT SOME DIFFERENT SHOTS." I replied, "Jesus Christ... when did they change the call time? Why didn't they announce it?" He replied, "THEY TOLD US LAST NIGHT AT THE BAR... MUST HAVE BEEN AFTER YOU LEFT." "Shit," I replied, "Who the fuck changes a Call Time after midnight?"

My mind was reeling. If I missed the camera look see, then I was as good as off Hamish's list of cam ops. This was NOT good. Bobby continued, "I'll TELL THEM THAT YOU'LL MEET US THERE

BUT YOU BETTER NOT MISS THE LOOK SEE. GOOD FUCKING LUCK BUDDY!" He then hung up.

We were continuing to motor down the river, cruising beneath its numerous street crossings and short bridges. I was fucked. People would be pissed. I faced losing two clients unless I could find a way to get to that Camera Meeting and look see. But how? We were quite a way along the river. The pier landing was well behind us.

The tour narration continued but my concentration was shot. What a position to be in! The city passed slowly above us, office buildings and skyscrapers. Then my phone buzzed again, stares of annoyance and condemnation from my fellow architecture lovers.

I answered the phone. It was the Production Manager's number and voice; she sounded irate. "JIM... WHERE ARE YOU? YOUR CALL TIME IS NOW... WHY AREN'T YOU HERE?" I began to seriously sweat. My defense of not being in the bar when the change was announced cut me no slack. "PLEASE GET TO THE VENUE AS SOON AS POSSIBLE. HAMISH IS GOING TO DO A CAMERA MEETING, AND HE EXPECTS YOU TO BE THERE. SO, BE THERE!" She rang off. Hadn't these people ever thought to call or message me, maybe ring my room... some more twenty-first century method of spreading the news rather than relying on word of mouth at a bar at midnight? What the fuck. No doubt whose fault it would be if my ass wasn't in a chair at that meeting.

Some of the bridges were low hanging. Maybe it would be possible to grab onto the crisscross of steel girders supporting the bridge and Jungle Jim it to the shore, then hail a cab? I'm no athlete though. The clock was ticking. That option vanished as soon as my higher reasoning powers were able to grasp cognitive thinking away from panic. The longer I delayed making a decision, the worse it would get. If I missed the meeting, there would be no hope of working for any of Hamish's upcoming shows... shows that win Emmy Awards.

I had an idea; it was a long shot, but my other options were zero. Putting my cell phone to my ear and faking a conversation, I worked my way through the closely positioned chairs and walked into the main cabin. The purser was at a table busily counting the day's proceeds. Walking directly up to him I said, "I'm sorry but I'm a doctor and my nurse just called me with an emergency. She wouldn't call me unless... ." I broke off and pretended to be speaking with someone "What are his stats? Blood pressure? OK... shit... I'll get there as soon as I can... try and stabilize him!" Then to the purser, "I MUST get off this ship as soon as possible... a man's life is at stake!" I wasn't kidding, it was my life! Now there was no way in hell anyone would mistake me for an MD... passing for a Lawn Doctor would be a stretch. The purser, in near panic, said, "WE CAN'T STOP THE BOAT... YOU CAN'T GET OFF." Putting the phone back to my ear and hoping it didn't ring to reveal my deceit, I barked into the phone again, "What are his stats now... ok shit... have Dr. Larson cover me until I can get off this boat!" The purser's face followed my conversation with worried interest. Then he said, "I'LL ASK THE CAPTAIN IF WE CAN LET YOU OFF!" I thanked him profusely.

Returning shortly, he said, "I CAN'T BELIEVE THIS... WE'RE GOING TO TURN AROUND AND RETURN TO THE DOCK... WE'VE NEVER DONE THIS BEFORE!" After making an announcement and apologizing to the other passengers, the boat did a U-Turn of sorts and returned to the dock. Was I ashamed of myself? I felt like an absolute piece of shit... but there was a decent chance that my ass would get to that goddamn Camera Meeting and yes, I had saved a man's life, his professional one at least.

The boat pulled up at the wharf. The deckhands removed a piece of the rail and made way for me to depart. Before I was able to take a step forward, a man strolled casually up to the opening, holding a smoking cigarette in his hand like a posing model, and stepped off the boat without saying a word. The deck hands began to replace the railing and I had to yell at them to stop. "I'm the doctor who has to get off!"

They replied, "THEN WHO THE HELL WAS THAT GUY?" I told them I had no idea. The show had sent a Production Assistant to pick me up and we raced to the venue. Bounding breathlessly up the stairs to where the Camera Meeting was supposed to be, I found an empty room. Panicking once again, I called Bobby D. "Where's the goddamn meeting now?" "CANCELED!" He said, "EVERYONE WENT TO LUNCH!"

If God was good to me there would not be laws in Chicago for impersonating a doctor. If there were such laws, maybe they would have a short Statute of Limitations, or I'd be going UP the river for a while and it wouldn't be for sightseeing.

Our second show was outstanding. The band had super high energy and once again my peers and I searched for memorable shots, competing against each other to receive as many bright red tally lights as we could and possibly even attain that coveted "ATTABOY!"

"PLEASE DON'T SHOOT ME MOM AND DAD"

2009

My work for HBO's premier boxing franchises BOXING AFTER DARK and WORLD CHAMPIONSHIP BOXING had taken me from Mexico and Las Vegas, to Boston, Houston, and Cancun. We had done programs in San Juan and Miami. Wherever rising fighters materialized, their promoters staged their matches. One other time though, we went to Tampa. This was a particular treat for me since my parents lived just north of the city. I would be able to spend my first night at their small home.

I liked to indulge myself with the pleasure of springing surprises on loved ones, especially my parents. Honestly though, my mom was considerably less pleased with my sudden appearances. My dad just rolled with the punches and I'm not sure he knew my visits were unexpected, not pre planned, and had not merely escaped his memory. My mom was constantly berating him for his forgetfulness, but it didn't faze him. He remembered meals, TV channel numbers, and where his favorite shows could be found, everything else could take its chances.

After I used my front door key to enter the house and heard my dad say, "Phyllis... somebody just came in... who THE FUCK is it... Phyllis... are we expecting anybody?" He shuffled out of his bedroom, his K-Mart slippers scuffing along the tile floor he thought was "too Goddamn cold on his bare feet," and then embraced me, laughing, and kissing my cheek with his scratchy perpetually day-old beard.

Mom rushed out to greet me and then I persuaded them to go out for dinner even though everyone knew "You couldn't trust restaurants!" After dinner we sat and talked for a while back in their kitchen. The recent run of shows and that day's travel had left me exhausted. They lived in a two-bedroom cinder block home and each of them had one room. There was only the long, wide sofa for guests to use in the Florida room, AKA the Lanai, which was fine with me. The garden variety development in which their home resided had been laid out, platted, and built in the 1960s. Their modest home was around twenty plus years old when they bought it.

The building fronted onto a storage pond maintained by the county. It was home to numerous species of birds and a small alligator or two, whom the other residents continued to feed despite the pleas of the game warden to not do so.

We played a game of Uno and then retired to sleep; they would both stay up watching TV in their respective bedrooms. My mom had complained that my father was constantly watching true crime dramas in which a guy kills his wife. Sometimes for cheating, for the insurance, or just because he's a prick and was tired of her voice or laugh. It didn't take a lot for some guys.

My dad called me into his eternally cluttered room. Its walls had photos and maps taped and stapled onto its walls, books were in piles and the TV blared... "Whatcha watching dad?" He responded, "Oh shit son, I don't know, some crime thing."

The narrator's voice was suitably dark and judgmental, "AFTER 30 YEARS OF MARRIAGE THE FIEND KILLED HER WHILE SHE SLEPT... WITHOUT REMORSE... THIRTY YEARS OF FAITHFULNESS AND COMPANIONSHIP MEANT NOTHING TO THIS MONSTER!" "That's pretty heavy shit dad." "What is son, oh that program? I've already seen this episode a few times." Christ, maybe mom was on to something.

My dad crossed the room, came close to me and after glancing down the very short hallway to my mom's bedroom, her door already closed, he motioned me to come closer. Whatever was about to happen was evidently not to be shared with my mom. In his right hand was a

.38 caliber revolver... his palsied fingers could barely hold the weapon level, it wavered and drooped in his trembling grasp. His left eye was nearly blind from cataracts and Macular Degeneration. He told me that there had been some neighborhood break-ins recently and felt they might need some protection. OK, I thought. As far as I knew dad had never been exactly a crack shot even with rifles. After thanking him for sharing the information, I set off toward the Lanai.

My mom's door creaked open... "Psssst Jimmie. Come here." I entered her bedroom, she glanced down the same short hallway and after confirming that my dad's door was closed, she eased her door shut. In her right hand was a .22-caliber pistol. WTF? "What's with the gun mom?" She was DEFINITELY not a crack shot. "I got it to protect myself in case your dad tries anything!" So this is what 55 years of marriage gets you? WTF? "Mom... ," I said. "I'm sure dad has no intention of killing you. Relax!" "Then why is he watching those true crime instructional videos on murdering your spouse?" I had no answer for that. Hugging and kissing her goodnight, I reassured her as best as I could, walked to the lanai and lay down on the comfortable sofa. There were photos of my siblings and I, our spouses and children on every flat surface and attached to the walls.

The Gulf of Mexico was so close that even with the mildest of onshore breezes, the scent of salty brine and rotting seaweed would drift through their yard. Flocks of wild birds squawked and croaked, tweeted and trilled while laughing gulls coasted noisily above, crying in their ceaseless search for food. It was riotously noisy, these squabbles over territory, nesting sites, and possible edibles there in the thick night. This circus was maybe 20 feet from where I lay as I was trying to block out the sounds in order to get some sleep. Something was screeching, I was trying to match the cries with the birds from my memory but not very successfully.

Either the birds gave up or my brain gave in but regardless, I must have fallen asleep because I awoke in the dark room. Only a few birds were still stirring. What was VERY active however was my bladder. I was about to flip off the covers and head to the toilet when I remembered that this was Mom and Dad's home. Two elderly people each alert for the slightest noise, each armed with loaded guns and the only toilet was in that same short and narrow hallway, between their bedrooms. My visit had been a complete surprise so neither of them might have any recollection that it was their grown son creeping through the hallway and not a scheming spouse or dangerous intruder.

I lay back down on the couch. Fumbling around in the lightless house might net me a few rounds of hot lead for my troubles. There was always the possibility that they would catch me in a crossfire. But I had to pee, and soon. Rising carefully and walking through the shadows of the dining room, I felt my way along the wall to their kitchen. Here there was some assistance from the moon whose soft illumination was enough for me to navigate through there and to the garage back door which creaked as my hand eased it open. Here it would be ok to switch on the overhead light.

There beneath the laundry sink was what I was hoping to find, the recycling bin. Searching delicately through the plastic bowls, foam containers and bottles, I found what was needed, a large steel coffee can, Maxwell House Regular Drip. It smelled of fresh brewed coffee and morning, which would soon be here! It even had a tight-fitting plastic lid! It would have to serve as my pissoir, and I counted myself very lucky. I could probably have gone outside but the neighbors' houses were very close. This being Florida, it was best to assume every house had weapons and a grown man in his underwear sneaking around through the oleanders and grapefruit trees at night was fair game.

All that remained for me to do was to advance across those wide-open floors, move through the shadows and hope not to bump, knock or nudge anything. Somewhere in there was mom's large ceramic elephant planter just waiting for me to make contact. Even the birds were quiet, possibly on edge expecting the bright flash and ear numbing blast of one or two guns to enliven the night. I imagined the NCIS Narrators voice over: "LITTLE DID THESE LOVING PARENTS REALIZE THAT THE FIGURE SKULKING THROUGH THEIR QUIET HOME WAS THEIR OWN SON. EACH FIRED REPEATEDLY AS THE OVERWEIGHT FIGURE SLUMPED TO THE TILE FLOOR, SHREDDED BY THE FUSILLADE. STAY TUNED FOR HUSBANDS WHO KILL!"

By comparison with my night, the next evening's heavyweight prize fight was relaxing with far less potential for an actual violent death.

GUNS N' ROSES

"**I** hit the mother fucker so hard his fucking eyes rolled back, he hit the sidewalk hard dude. I... thought I killed the mother fucker... funny as shit!"

The two street types were boasting and loitering, each sipping from the same tall boy poking up from the crumpled paper bag they passed between them. Neither seemed to notice me as I entered the door into the old theater. I had been booked to shoot Guns N' Roses. They were a West Coast metal band gaining traction based on the frequent air play of "SWEET CHILD OF MINE," which I really liked until the radio stations played it to death, turning it to audio wallpaper as they had "STAIRWAY TO HEAVEN," by Led Zeppelin.

This performance at The Ritz Theater would be the earliest stop on their APPETITE FOR DESTRUCTION 176 show tour... a grueling schedule but you must "strike while the iron is hot," as the saying goes.

For this show, I had been assigned a handheld camera position on the right side of the stage. It will be a busy night. The show was a sold-out full house. The band had already built an enthusiastic fan base and NYC loves live performances. A small area had been set aside for me and my utility guy, who would basically feed me my camera cable and prevent it from entangling my feet. Unfortunately for him, he would be down with the crowd who were already pushing toward the stage. A shallow protective barricade would keep him safe and give me someplace to exit to if the band began to use the full stage.

As a rule, the cam ops never get between the performer and their fans... ever. Roadies and even the artists themselves have been known to shove intrusive camera operators off the stage, sometimes literally, if they become particularly abusive of the stage space. One of my camera buddies, after being shoved by one of the BEASTIE BOYS, threw the offending singer off the stage. Mike was the wrong guy to mess with.

I squatted in position waiting for the band to appear. My camera was resting on my shoulder, I was safely out of anyone's way. The packed audience was already compressing and surging forward as more people entered the crowded theater. Promoters would eagerly sell seats in the air if they could! One couple drew my attention because the guy was eyeing me and seemed to be scowling. He was with an unusually tall girl who reminded me of the Daryl Hannah replicant in "BLADE RUNNER." White, blonde hair shocked into a mane, her eyes rimmed black with eyeshadow, and lips red as a vampire's heart. The boyfriend drew deeply on a hand rolled fatty. Its tip flared a fiery bright red with each pull. Even from my perch onstage, the pungent aroma reached me; it was strong dope, maybe home grown. He offered it to his female companion, who took a long hit. She then threw her linen white neck back and howled... just your average She Wolf. When she thrust her fashionably thin arms above her head, there was a line of dirt in the crease of the armpit, as though drawn by an indelible marker through the pinkish stubble.

The headliners hadn't even taken the stage yet, she was losing it to house music. It was going to be a long night. Eventually, the band wandered on stage in no particular hurry. They began with a muscular power chord that ignited the audience into deafening cheers and screams. The force of sound from the amps made my clothing vibrate. I pushed the spongy ear plugs deeper into my ears. The crowd rolled like a wave breaking against the immovable stage. Glancing at my utility guy, I could see he was safe, eyes watching me intently, my wingman.

My primary responsibility was Slash, their impressive lead guitarist. Axl Rose, the lead singer, began his rocking, writhing, and dancing, his signature bandana in place. The very strong rhythm section followed their lead. Slash wove his inventive, melodic guitar lines through each song, always sharp, promising more. The band cruised through song after song. Working hard, wanting to impress NYC. Axl sometimes rushed my camera, closed with Slash into an intimate "see what buddies we two are" shot. The pace was relentless and exciting. I scurried back and forth across the lip of the stage, always following Slash, certainly never leading. My blood raced as I continuously framed and reframed shots, searching for that vital glance, smile, or even sneer that would make that single shot work. Feeling great when the tiny red tally light blinked on, indicating the Director's approval, the "Attaboy", immediately rejoining the hunt for the next best shot once the light left. The cam ops were constantly competing against each other, chasing the elusive tally light as though it was Harry Potter's Quidditch ball. Seven or more of us working simultaneously and only one of us at a time could be right.

Somewhere around the seventh song, on one of my stage crosses, a hand grabbed at my leg, which caused me to topple. It was She Wolf's boyfriend. I guessed he had had his fill of my blocking his view. My knees slammed onto the polished hardwood stage, immediately opening a wound from another recent concert. Before I could regroup, the Director took my camera. I had fallen while framing a head to toe shot of Slash, whose body filled my lens. The red tally flashed on, a judgmental eye, with its momentary approval likely to vanish at any second. The pressure was on.

The band had begun "PARADISE CITY," and the audience went wild. Zooming my lens as wide as it would go, I framed Slash, who forced me onto my back with his rapid approach and ever-present top hat balanced on his head like a Mad Hatter armed with a guitar. He stared down through dark glasses, forcing me to lie down flat, between my knees. The white-hot light from the folo-spots blasted him, other lights bathed him with ambers and reds from the side while flaring back lights outlined his tall, black clad figure.

He blitzed the guitar's neck with a frenzied deluge of notes, driving the song's relentless beat, deft fingers moving too fast to follow. Sweat drops fell from his face, glittering in the light, hitting my hands and camera. Drifts of oily smoke from the foggers floated across the stage, crossing through shafts of stage lighting. The compact mass seemed to move as one dense, vibrating creature. The crowd was intense, emitting ceaseless screams and yells as it pressed ever more forward, undoubtedly crushing She Wolf and her stoned consort, like overripe fruit.

Slash broke away, the tally left but returned as I captured Axl in a waist shot, approaching me with reptilian bends and sways, his face a screaming mask of red intensity, microphone to his lips. Briefly, the action moved further away from me. I was sweating; my clothes matted to my skin. The cloth bandana tied around my forehead to keep the sweat out of my eyes drooped, limp and soaked. My eyes stung and the camera viewfinder eyepiece fogged up as soon as I brought my face to it.

This was it baby, one of the most exciting jobs in the world. Being not just onstage with a powerhouse like Guns N' Roses but also working with them to create something new, a joint collaboration. I was savoring extra-long tallies, milking every second of the shot, anticipating my next move. Following the band's antics, letting them lead me to great shots, reveling when they worked and discarded shots once they fell apart, always chasing and watching, composing on the fly, real run N gun.

The show finally ended. The band left the stage without the usually obligatory encores audiences had come to expect. The Director thanked the crew; Producers called a wrap. My utility assistant took the overheated camera from my right shoulder which itself was hot to the touch, abused and swollen. My shoulders relaxed. The knot of tension at the base of my neck throbbed. When I touched my knee, the blood from the reopened cut stained my fingers through the black fabric.

The crowd headed for the exits. It would take me a full 90 minutes to drive home. I would need every minute of that time for the adrenaline to diminish and the ringing in my ears to subside. Some of the crew headed to an East Village bar, some to lit joints and a few would end up doing both.

With the car windows open to the night's cool breeze, my head began to clear. I had already changed into a dry shirt. Tomorrow my assignment was a concert with Cheryl Crow at an uptown theater. No mosh pit and an afternoon call time.

Thank God. Sweet Child of Mine!

EMMY

My first Emmy Award almost slipped right by me. I didn't even know that our show had been nominated, that we had won, or frankly anything else about the nominating process or how shows ended up in competition for this prestigious award. I was clueless. Please be gentle as I have a very steep learning curve about almost everything.

These were the days before "TMZ" and TWITTER. My days were not spent watching "ACCESS HOLLYWOOD" or browsing through the trade papers. When opportunities and shows came my way, I accepted or declined, depending on my circumstances. Our show never notified me that the camera operators had been nominated for Individual Achievements recognition. That is the only way the cam ops ever got to embrace that svelte, highly polished gold body and call her our own.

A show's Producers nominate their show themselves. So do each of the various departments such as Audio, Makeup and Hair, Editing, Musical Score, Director, etc. If you do not nominate yourself then your particular skill or craft will not enter into competition... no entry, no award. Each nominee is judged by a group of their peers. Only 5 of the hundreds of shows produced annually can be nominated per category. One year I received nominations for the GRAMMY AWARDS, ROLLING STONES LIVE ON HBO, and ROBIN WILLIAMS ON BROADWAY.

Three out of 5. Better than even odds that I would win. Friends have been nominated for 4 and even 5 of the shows at one time. Four nominations is no guarantee, 5 means make room on the fireplace mantle. Even being a part of such high visibility productions with major stars was not enough. My 3 shows lost to Cher.

It is possible for the show itself to win but none of the individuals or departments. It happens. For my first show nomination, someone had carelessly left my name off the list of camera operators supplied to the National Academy of Television Arts and Sciences - NATAS. After the awards ceremony, the Academy declined to award me my statue. It was only through the intercession of the well-respected Technical Director, Keith Weinkopf, that the Academy relented and approved my award after he vouched for the contribution made by me to the show. Thanks Keith. Alas, my statue was crushed in the Northridge Earthquake. Poor Emmy, thankfully, there was a replacement waiting "in the wings!"

To add to the confusion, there are separate awards for PRIMETIME and DAYTIME shows. To receive a nomination in either category is an honor but PRIMETIME gets most of the media attention. It's where the A List stars are. This is the show that most people watch on Network television. Technical awards are distributed at an earlier date and are recorded but not broadcast. The award ceremony is held in Hollywood.

There are stars in attendance at our technical awards ceremony also but fewer of them. They might be headlining the cast of the program and are there to show their support. Name stars are also chosen to act as hosts. To the nominees, it really doesn't matter, it's wonderfully exciting anyway. It's far more important that we get to be there knowing that we are being recognized for excellence by our industry peers.

For my first two wins I had decided not to attend the ceremony. There was airfare, hotel, car and tuxedo rentals to consider, I needed to save some money. It wasn't until the "RACHAEL RAY SHOW" was nominated that I bit the bullet and took my wife and two children to Los Angeles for the event.

It was Rachael's first season for her show and the camera operators and Technical Director had received nominations. It's good to have the muscle of a Network behind you. Nevertheless, the camera operators and our Technical Director were dumbstruck that our show had been included.

If you're up against a category killer like the OLYMPICS or a live production like "ANNIE," you might as well save your money. When first approached by the Producers, we conferenced together to pick one of our episodes to submit for consideration. Then we sent that particular show off to the National Academy of Television Arts and Sciences (NATAS). After that, it was in God's hands. The episode we chose might have been completely different from one chosen by any of the other departments.

We considered our chances. It was a plus that ours was a first season show. Rachael was attractive and very popular, another plus. We also had the influence and power of the CBS Network behind us which was a very big plus, but not enough to guarantee a win.

None of the other operators chose to go so we would have our own table. My wife and kids were absolutely thrilled at the prospect of a trip to California. They're veteran travelers and love getaways. It would be a great vacation even if our show lost.

We flew to Los Angeles, arriving well after midnight. The kids were younger then and so sleep deprived they were singing, dancing, and acting goofy. Every parent knows what comes next! The apartment I had reserved was locked, it was very late and there was no one around to give us entry. After calling the contact number given to me, a very sleepy but surprisingly calm man arrived and opened the door for us. The kids barely made it to their beds before collapsing. On the following morning we drove to Hollywood so I could get the final fitting for my rented tuxedo. My wife and daughter had each bought fashionable evening dresses and my son, a new suit. We wanted to look as great as we felt.

You know all of those "discovery" stories that have fed the Hollywood dream machine for decades? The tales of salesgirls, pool guys, and other commoners catching the attention of some talent scout or casting director? They are not entirely bullshit. Case in point. We would need to wait for my tux to be tailored. It was supposed to be a quick fix. On the counter of the tailor's shop was an advertisement for a "Headshot" package. $100 got you the complete deal: several 8 x 10 black and white glossies plus a contact sheet with various poses. Since both of our children were attractive and photogenic, I suggested to my wife that we buy a package for our son as his younger sister was not interested. These headshots are what casting directors use to pick candidates for commercials, films, and television shows. Each candidate has thousands of headshots and most of the photos will not get their subjects 10 minutes in the industry.

The phone number for the advertised offer was answered by a man who came right over. We asked him questions; he met both kids and then took off with our son.

It's hard to say which one of us had the first "WHAT THE FUCK" inkling that we had allowed our child to go off with a strange man to be "photographed!" The nearby San Fernando Valley was America's porn industry capitol. We didn't know anything about the affable photographer. My wife was giving me a definite, "This was your idea look." We agreed mutually that our respective mothers did not need to know about this part of our LA adventure. God help my son if my spur of the moment suggestion was wrong.

In about 45 minutes, the man returned with our son who did not seem at all flustered, frightened or nervous. He and the photographer were laughing together as his car drove up. The man then asked if either of our children had agents representing them. My wife and I were a little stunned, if such a condition was even possible. Talk about WTF moments! I told him we were in town for the Emmys, the kids had only had about 6 hours of sleep in two days, my tuxedo was being altered, and no, they did not have agents. He asked us if we would mind if he made a few phone calls to people he knew. We saw no harm in this. What did we have to lose? He cautioned us that he could guarantee us nothing. We laughed and said we understood. He would call us later in the day if he was able to work anything out. That was it. We said our goodbyes and parted.

Three hours later as we were cruising Van Nuys, he called. Each of the kids had auditions scheduled for the following day with a casting agency representing Nickelodeon and Disney, among others. Just like that, lightning struck our confused children and bewildered us. Hollywood lightning baby, the very best kind. Elapsed time since our arrival in LA, around 11 hours, and we had auditions lined up already.

Mommy and daddy were both industry veterans, we had met on the "NEW MICKEY MOUSE CLUB" when it was being shot in Orlando. We cautioned the kids that auditions were great but that did not mean that they might be working in film or television anytime soon and probably never at all, but they should still feel honored and very, VERY lucky. Other kids received extensive acting, voice, and dance lessons, had personal agents, resumes, and made annual pilgrimages to Los Angeles during Pilot Season hoping to get a shot at a series, or anything. Most went back to their hometowns with nothing to show but maxed out charge cards.

Both kids seemed to be taking the situation in stride. It was us, the parents, who were struggling to come to terms with what exactly might be going on. To say we were flummoxed would not be an exaggeration. In fact, neither one of us was even sure we wanted our kids exposed to careers in entertainment. We had each spent time working on auditions and knew the anxiety and heartache that thrives in the business; the terrible insecurity feeding on performer's self-esteem and self-image, novice or veteran, young or old.

My wife had sat in on the auditions for Disney's MOUSE CLUB revamp. She was there when Christina Aguilera, Justin Timberlake,

Brittany Spears, Ken Russell, JC Chavez, Ryan Gosling, Lindsay Ailey and a score of immensely talented, bright young things were paraded before Disney executives and expected to perform and impress. This they did, but many others did not. Looks and talent alone are simply not enough, not even close. You also need luck and sometimes, a lightning strike. That much, we had. It was a promising start.

I'm pretty sure that the kids slept better than their parents, speaking for myself anyhow. We drove to the Chateau Marmont to have breakfast in their garden. It was the beginning of a family tradition. Each time an Emmy nomination comes my way now, we begin Awards day there at the Chateau, legendary haunt of Golden Age stars, rogues, starlets and Hollywood's elite. The Chateau is where Errol Flynn bedded leading lady wannabes and where John Belushi died. The breakfast was excellent and yes, you can still enjoy star sightings there. We certainly have. Just be cool... no staring, selfies, or autographs. Just act like you belong there and perhaps one day, you will.

The four of us sat together in the Agency's waiting room, its walls laden with framed photos of numerous young stars. Other kids were scattered in the luxurious chairs around the room and our kids were excited to recognize some of them from the shows they watched. Like a doctor's office, assistants came out and escorted each of our kids into other rooms. Each of them read separately for commercials. Our exhausted daughter was in no condition for such a test, but we had no control over the situation. We waited anxiously for their return not sure what results we should expect, or if they would say anything at all. Nor were we sure what we hoped those results would be.

The agent who had contacted us said the consensus was that our daughter was a little too young and both kids had ZERO experience. The Agent suggested that our son audition for local theater, get some experience, and then get another audition with their New York City office. It was politely explained to us that neither of our children could realistically be "sold" to Directors, who had neither the time nor inclination to "train" a would-be performer. It all made perfect sense and was not exactly a surprise.

We left the agency with a sense of relief. It was time to prepare for tonight's ceremony. We negotiated our way along Sunset Boulevard. A popular song by the Country Pop group Rascal Flatts came on the radio as our car approached the hotel. That was an interesting sign as Rachael Ray loved the song and the audio guys would play it for her before each show, to psyche her up. Was this a good omen?

As I searched for a parking spot, Janie and the kids went up to our room. The girls always appreciated a head start. My intention was to give them as much time as possible. After parking nearby and dawdling for a while, it was time for me to begin laying out my tuxedo. The elevator took me to our floor. The maid's cart was sitting there in the empty hallway. The name tag attached to the cart said EMMY. This must surely be a good omen! When I told the family about this unusual coincidence, they became very excited. Janie and Reilly looked absolutely gorgeous. Aidan had squeezed into his new suit with all the finesse that a skateboarder used to baggy shorts could muster. Now it was my turn. Rented tuxedos always have surprises like missing buttons, waistbands that will neither expand nor contract and other little challenges to deal with. Yet here was another positive omen. This tuxedo was perfect; nothing missing or ill fitting. The waist buttons were a little loose but nothing to worry about.

We left for the Dolby Theater. Los Angeles had been very, very good to us so far. What more could we reasonably expect? The area around the theater was a mass of spectators. Our Lyft turned into the line of cars which were creeping through the security barriers. The driver seemed both unnerved and excited by all the attention given to his car. Bomb sniffing dogs walked its perimeter, intimidating security types peered inside at us, and once they had approved our tickets, we were waved through. The driver giggled with relief. As we left our ride and joined the crowd of attendees in their evening attire, the eyes of hopeful fans scoured everyone looking for famous faces.

Janie was born with attractive good looks; her mother was a model on "THE PRICE IS RIGHT." She and our daughter, who inherited that natural attractiveness, both looked radiant and some of the more curious fans took photos of them just in case. They certainly looked like "someone" even if their images might be deleted later in some more sober, post ceremony culling. They were certainly "someone" to me.

We picked up our programs and walked along the red carpet in front of the representatives of the various press and media outlets. Correspondents were doing live reports, their backs to us, while news camera crews and radio reporters scoured our slow-moving groups looking for the notable and famous. Even Janie and our daughter did not attract any attention from this unimpressed, "been there/seen this" group of professionals. We were excited and thrilled just to be there that it didn't matter to any of us. We entered the auditorium where tables had been set up for the various shows and their nominees, found our spots and settled in.

This year's hosts were three of the stars from NBC's hit show "THE OFFICE." The actors who played Kevin, Angela, and Oscar were the entire staff of the fictional Accounting Department. The show was one of our favorites. We had seen every episode repeatedly. Having them be in the same room with my family made the event even more memorable.

Unfortunately for me, the rented tuxedo began to misbehave. Not that it's a big problem mind you, just the goddamn clothing I was wearing! The buttons holding my pants waist together both came off. OK, I know what you're thinking, "This guy must be severely weight challenged." Nay, the threads were loose when I first fastened them, but not yet cause for panic. It was the eleventh hour anyway, what could I do? It would not be a problem unless our show won, as improbable as that seemed. The sketchy cummerbund would suffice for the moment.

We scanned the program to see where my award category was placed in the ceremony order. Award after award was announced to general applause from the crowded room and absolute pandemonium from the winner's groups. I can't truthfully say that I was indifferent as we watched other winners make the perp walk up to the stage. Our Category was next in line. Just to be safe, I repeated my pre-prepared acceptance speech to myself. Following the last forkful of the delicious dessert, and with the teacup at my lips, my studied nonchalance collapsed when my wife and kids began screaming. Attendees at surrounding tables turned to look at us and began applauding. Rachael's show had won. After hugging my family, I began my walk through the crowd. Our table was not close to the stage, a searchlight was blinding me, it was an endless journey. Strangers patted me on my arm and back, nominees at other tables who knew me yelled out my name and the rented tuxedo pants finally gave way. The waistband popped open, forcing me to continue walking with one hand clutching my pants, perilously close to making Emmy Award history as the "WINNER WHO ACCEPTED THE AWARD IN HIS UNDERWEAR." That would surely merit coverage from the assorted news crews who had ignored us earlier and were now recording this ceremony. After arriving at the podium, I began my acceptance speech, remembering to thank the Academy, Rachel, the Producers, the Director, my family, my parents, our camera assistants, and the other cameramen.

When the Statuette was placed in my left hand, my right was still grasping my sliding pants in a white knuckled death grip. Then it was over. The audience continued to applaud me as I headed for the wings where a group of officials were smiling in welcome and steered me to a "photo op" position before pointing me back into the comparative darkness of the theater. Envious eyes watched as Emmy and I made the return walk to our table. The audience was already applauding the next winner who had begun her walk to fame. My sweaty palms handed off the gleaming statue to my children. It was now possible for me to release the hold on my pants to let them do and go where they might.

The following morning was just your average sunny beginning to a day in Los Angeles. We had decided to take a TOUR OF THE STARS HOMES and boarded a silly looking safari style vehicle decked out with plastic weedy fringe around its top. The driver was wearing cargo shorts and a cartoonish great white hunter pith helmet as we set off to hunt for stars here in wildest Hollywood.

The other tourist passengers would certainly keep their eyes sharp to spot those elusive "A Listers" lurking amid the lush lawns, adobe style mansions, and sky-blue pools here in their natural habitat. We rolled along Hollywood Boulevard. In a fit of residual excitement from the previous evening, my wife announced to the occupants of our jungle vehicle that they were riding with an actual Emmy winner. There were gasps and applause. Heads turned to stare and smile at me with degrees of interest ranging from "How exciting" to "Who gives a royal shit."

Somewhere on the Boulevard, we stopped at a traffic light. I had been contentedly savoring the pleasure of being a three-time Emmy winner, feeling proud, mentally picturing the row of gold-plated beauties soon to be arrayed on my mantle at home. Absent-mindedly, my gaze fell on a street-side cafe. A young guy sat there with 3 beautiful girls: ah Hollywood.

He watched with interest as we rolled to a stop. His skeptical eyes took in the jungle jeep, sketchy fringe of plastic green weeds, our pith helmeted driver and his cargo of open-mouthed tourists gaping at the passing scene with excitement and anticipation.

Flashing a snarky smile, he hugged two of the girls into a tighter circle, said something to them and then the group turned to look and laugh at us. They radiated all of the mocking contemptuous amusement that young, self-assuredly beautiful people are capable of. My Emmy daydream faded. No one else in our vehicle had noticed them.

The guy then pointed directly at me, cupped his right hand, and began to stroke the empty air as though masturbating. OK, I get it, I'm a jerk off. Averting my gaze to stare at this goddamn interminable traffic light, I foolishly turned to look at our critics again. The four of them were rocked with laughter. I just knew in my heart that if these kids realized that I was an actual Emmy Award winner, their mockery would change to admiration. If only I had brought Emmy and after removing her from the satin covered base in the protective travel case, raised her high into the Hollywood sunlight, they would envy her hard, rounded ass, her outstretched arms, wings, and the smooth rise of her nipple-less breasts.

My enemies would be smitten, their laughter turning to nods of approval and admiration. Unfortunately, my secret weapon was locked away in the cargo bay of a FedEx flight.

The light remained stubbornly RED. In a moment of masochistic weakness, my head turned towards Lothario and his luscious posse. I didn't really mind the guy but there was something especially disconcerting about the beautiful young women laughing at me. A part of my pride and spirit had taken a nasty hit. The years had flown by.

He wasn't done with me yet, a feral cat playing with a mortally wounded creature, he eyed me carefully and with a smirk, began to slide his hand to and fro into his open mouth while his tongue probed its cheek. Now I was a blow job. The girls nearly fell from their chairs with contortions of laughter. They rocked back and forth, their lustrous hair tossed in the morning sunlight, eyes tearing behind their designer sunglasses. His work done, the guy sat back contentedly, the light finally turned green and onward we went. By that time I had already been bagged and trophied.

As they say, shit happens. No matter what the young people thought of our little tour group, we were having fun and embracing the excitement of this marvelous city. We loved the weather, the driver was one of those "Although I'm driving this crappy jeep, I'm actually an actor, etc." types and his charming narration kept us interested and even laughing.

The young critics still had their lives ahead of them. With hard work and luck, no, basically connections and luck, better make it just connections, the right doors might open for them someday. They certainly had for me. I was a recognizable name in a fabulous profession that had brought me awards, travel, numerous friends, and exciting experiences. It had brought me a beautiful wife and family.

I had arrived at a place in life that I could not have imagined when I was their age. My youthful confusion and anxieties were long gone and if they were lucky, those young people might get to where I found myself that gorgeous morning, admiring the homes of the wealthy and famous, without suffering an ounce of envy or regret.

During the afternoon we drove to Malibu Beach. We had lunch at Paradise Cove and watched as the kids jumped and cavorted in the Pacific while a curious seal pup approached and kept them company.

On our return, we drove through the canyons on winding, narrow roads carved out of the hills and perched above creek beds that glistened in the distance below us. The occasional eagle would glide on the thermal's high overhead, rulers of the bright blue California sky.

EMMY would rejoin us back at our home in a day or two. During the open windowed drive, Randy Newman's song "I LOVE LA" came on the radio. We couldn't have agreed with him more!

LUCIANO PAVAROTTI

A h, those glorious tenors with their stock in trade, beautiful operatic arias, duets, and Neapolitan love songs. Before gangs of rogue tenors began to prowl high end popular culture, sell out stadiums and throw a lifeline to PBS Pledge Week, there was Pavarotti, Placido and late crooner, Andrea Bocelli. Throughout the 80s, 90s, and aughts, these talented troubadours virtually ruled the popular classical world. Each of them had transitioned from the world's largest, most esteemed opera houses with their rarified air of the highbrow and precious, to apply their considerable vocal talents to more common and accessible compositions, the street songs of Naples, romantic ballads, and even Christmas albums.

It had been my great pleasure to work with each of these artists many times in many venues, but please allow me to reminisce about a few extracurricular encounters that occurred far from the hallowed halls of the Met or La Scala.

A video arts special had booked me to shoot an interview with Pavarotti, The Great One himself at the pied a terre he kept on Manhattan's Upper West Side. It was located in a large and very fashionable apartment complex. An assistant confided to me that Maestro used the quarters as a place to work with his "students". He threw me a conspiratorial "just between we guys look", wink and leered knowingly.

The rest of the crew and production staff arrived early enough to set up our lights and cameras. Soon we were joined by the Art Director and his staff. They carried arms full of vibrantly colored fresh flowers in dramatic shapes, sizes and hues that practically screamed, "NOTICE ME!" Along with these Summertime bouquets, they had picked up some object d'art, suitably exotic statues, and eye-catching fabrics, all necessary to create or enhance the to be expected impression of a great artist's home.

Sometimes, celebrities have remarkable pedestrian and common personal taste when choosing their home decor. Success in life does not necessarily translate into a connoisseur's appreciation of art and sculpture, in short, great taste! Their private homes would not live up to the fantasies of fans and viewers. They chose to live in the personally comfortable, rather than exist in alien surroundings chosen and arranged by strangers, no matter how erudite and fashionable they might be. Many other celebrities were quite at ease hiring whichever interior decorator was currently in vogue and were happy to nestle within whatever decor was chosen by them.

Many years ago, I had often worked at the Chase Manhattan Bank headquarters in New York's Financial District. David Rockefeller, a well-respected, ultra-wealthy, and very serious art collector, was the bank's Chairman. If our shoot was to be with him, an assistant would precede his boss, inspecting whatever offices Rockefeller intended to walk through. The personal photos and mementos of the desk workers, stray artwork and God forbid, posters, were removed. Any colors that David disliked, it was said that he had such refined taste that certain colors made him nauseous, were also banished. The offices were visually sanitized.

Not everyone could afford a personal decor stylist. Pavarotti obviously could, but in keeping with the assistant's description of the apartment, there was virtually nothing personal on display. It was evident Luciano did not spend much time there. Frankly, it did not appear as if the apartment had any inhabitants.

The Art Department went immediately to work transforming the corporate looking interior into the abode of a bon vivant world citizen with Old World European style and panache. In short, they ladled good taste on nearly every surface in our chosen location, the living room. Drab upholstery was enlivened with a beautiful piece of fabric as casually draped as something deliberately placed, can be. Throw pillows in the colors and designs of Middleastern and Native American blankets added just that bit of the exotically foreign, even for a foreigner. The price tags were left on but hidden so everything could be returned to whatever Home Decor store the goods had come from. Lifeless corners of the background might get a potful of crimson geraniums or an elaborate palm tree. The geraniums could not be returned but someone would make good use of them. The palm was plastic and tagged, bound for the returns desk.

The trick was to create the illusion of refined taste without allowing the statues, plants, or fabrics to draw attention away from the interviewee; nothing should compete for the eye's attention everything should blend harmoniously while confirming the sophistication and taste of our guest.

Once the set was ready, we just needed to wait for Pavarotti. With my camera in position and ready to go, there was a little time for me to relax. My first desire was to use the bathroom. The commode and its environs had nothing personal about them. No magazine casually set aside; no damp towel draped over the shower door. The harsh light and nearly blank walls were the face of sterility itself. Pavarotti did keep a small number of toilet articles around the sink top, all carefully arranged. A comb, toothbrush, and a bottle of cologne was part of the collection.

Being naughty and unprofessional, I picked up the cologne and gave my wrists a polite spritz. It was Vetiver, a delicious scent. A short blast went to my neck. How often does one get to savor an expensive scent, on the house, or part of it anyhow? Pavarotti would not miss what I had, out of true respect, borrowed from him.

The Great One arrived and after looking at the new decor, said nothing, he took his seat with an air of indifference and slight impatience. This interview seemed more like an imposition than an exposition. He looked at my camera and with an authoritarian reprimand, ordered me to move it to a more flattering angle. The ABC Lighting Director told him that this would not be an easy adjustment to make. It would mean moving his lights in addition to my camera. Accepting that such a reposition would take quite a bit of time, he agreed to allow me to slide my camera to a more frontal shot, which was done. We were now ready to begin recording.

I could smell the scent of Pavarotti's cologne on my skin. It's not every day that a plebe like me can, with the flick of a finger, achieve European sophistication and gentlemanly refinement. For a few brief minutes, Pavarotti and I would inhabit the same olfactory plane, we would smell, reasonably, alike. I felt sublime and exulted in the richness of the fragrance. Before we started the tape rolling, I noticed that the collar on Pavarotti's shirt was bent. After receiving permission from the Director to fix the collar, I reached over to adjust the shirt. He slowly turned his large head and sniffed at my arm. He seemed confused and then gave me a quizzical look. He had come to a conclusion and did not appear happy. He must have smelled his cologne on my wrist. We rolled tape, he was cued to speak and instantly, his bearded face erupted into a toothy, generous, soul of the South grin. All Neapolitan charm, both friendly and seductive. He was "walking through it" as we say. He could have phoned it in. There was a bit of the "Aren't we lucky to be alive and doing this crappy little interview that no one will ever see" compliance to him. He or his agent had agreed to it and here he was.

Our show host was a lovely woman, that alone was enough to hold his interest. He made good eye contact with her. Sometimes he would turn to look away as if favoring the unseen audience with his conviviality and abundant charm and sometimes, at other times he made eye contact directly with me, personally. The Director began to ask, "What is he looking at? Stage manager, what is he looking at... is someone distracting him?" It was no secret to me what Pavarotti was looking at. As the lights made the room hotter, and with the air conditioning shut off to appease the sound man, my skin warmed, then glistened with a sheen of sweat. The Vetiver had kicked into high gear.

It occurred to me that he must be thinking, "If this camera guy can afford my cologne, it's time to get a new scent!" Mercifully, in all of the post interview confusion and bustling about, he never confronted me about this remarkable coincidence. Once my camera was boxed and ready to be returned to the video truck, I made as scentless an exit as possible and hurried into the night, wondering if Macy's perfume counter had the same cologne and if I could afford a small bottle. It occurred to me that I rather liked the smell of greatness.

PLACIDO DOMINGO

Pavarotti was an operatic artist of the popular imagination; he was a cloaked figure wearing a Belle Epoque hat at a rakish angle, appearing directly from La Boehme. In person, I found him to be less personable than Placido, too self-consciously the Artiste, Domingo was more likable, perhaps more accessible. Although I very much enjoyed the Italian brio, and Pavarotti's vernacular, Neapolitan Street songs, he remained the unapproachable "Opera Star - hard to imagine him walking anywhere without making an Entrance." Cue applause. Nevertheless, what a beautiful lyrical voice. I had done many shows with "Pav," as we lovingly referred to him on headsets.

Placido had, arguably, a more powerful voice and was the more dramatic singer. Both men performed often at New York's Metropolitan Opera. I had never worked with either star outside of that venue or Lincoln Center.

I had been booked on a Lincoln Center for The Performing Arts Special production entitled, "STEPPIN OUT WITH THE LADIES." Domingo romanced and entertained numerous female stars circa 1980s fame. In gowns that glittered and gleamed, stars like Juliet Prowse, Leslie Uggams, Susan Anton, and others stared adoringly at Placido as he performed on stage. A couple of them threw roses of appreciation at the singer in his operatic costume.

As much a love letter to New York City, Placido did a walking tour complete with fountains, carriage rides, and glowing commentary. Following the brief travelog, he sang and danced with his female companions in individual, non-operatic performance pieces. Domingo was younger, more agile, and considerably thinner than Pavarotti. It was corny, but it charmed and was successful.

I worked on both parts of the show shot in the theater and those recorded at other locations. The show was beautiful, a romance saturated bonbon. The last section I shot involved Placido dancing with his co-stars in a foggy, dreamscape, moving them gracefully through the mist, accompanied by a melodic score.

It was winter and I had arrived at the West Side studio location wearing my brand-new parka. The location was buzzing with activity. The Art Director was in a panic because this did not arrive or that did not look right. Wardrobe was arranging the ladies' gowns and Placido's outfit. I hung my coat on a wall hook and after setting my camera up, readied to begin shooting. We rehearsed the choreography without fog at first. When everyone was satisfied with their area of responsibility, the stars departed to wardrobe and the prop technicians began to smoke up the set.

The overzealous prop guys had filled the entire large studio with the oil-based smoke. Think London around 1888, I pictured a Bobby or Sherlock Holmes appearing from out of the mist instead of Placido with a beautiful woman. The smoke leaves a slimy residue on surfaces and gives anyone who breathes it for too long, nasty "smoke boogers and sneezes that are inky black."

After a couple of hours inhaling the smoke, I found myself beginning to hyperventilate. I figured it might be best to walk outside the studio and get some wintery, Midtown air. At the place where I had hung up my new coat, there was an empty hook. The coat had vanished. It wasn't likely it was stolen, but its absence was odd, nonetheless. I went outside anyway but did not stay long. Searching for the coat proved fruitless. Then it was back to work.

While one of our lady dancers was doing a last second wardrobe adjustment, a sudden burst of laughter drew my attention to a group of women sitting toward the back of the studio. It was the makeup, hair, and wardrobe staff. They were clustered around an older woman whom I recognized as the show's script writer. Married to a powerful

Theater Producer who wielded a lot of influence on Broadway, she had said something that amused her admirers. The source of the hilarity was the writer's little poodle. The precious little thing, ribbons, and all, was nestled comfortably in the hood of my parka. The writer laughingly said, "I don't know who owns this coat but they will probably be annoyed!" What a clever fucking line. She did not want her poodle's white fur stained by any of the smoke grease that covered the floor. I was furious but knew that making a stink about the issue might cause trouble between the studio owners and the Producers, so I kept my temper. As soon as fur ball got up to wander, I walked over and picked up the coat, placing it on my camera. The posse of women became immediately silent.

The people who owned the studio thanked me for controlling my anger and offered to have the coat cleaned. The writer was obviously an intelligent woman and used to running in sophisticated company yet lacked any common decency. She never apologized but I've outlived her and her poodle, so I guess that's what they call the last laugh.

ANDREA BOCELLI

In retrospect, I do not believe my professional career crossed paths with Bocelli until we both ended up on a PBS Pledge Week during a wonderful summer evening in the 1990s. There was a concert at Liberty Park in New Jersey within sight of the Statue of Liberty where she still stands in New York Harbor watching for the "teeming masses" who are now reduced to crawling, swimming, and sneaking into our country through its southern "service entrance." The welcome mat has been rolled up and put into storage, indefinitely. I was not on a "game camera" here as the Director had never used me before. My assignment was to shoot hosts who would ask for pledges at minimally intrusive moments during the evening's performance.

Bocelli would be performing both singly and in duets with the English singer Sarah Brightman. Their recording of "TIME TO SAY GOODBYE" was then getting the airplay enjoyed by "FREEBIRD," "HOTEL CALIFORNIA," and "STAIRWAY TO HEAVEN" on less highbrow radio stations. It certainly was a lovely song.

Throughout the night, our hosts would discretely interrupt the music in order to dun viewers for pledges of financial support intended to keep this show and similar programs available for free. In fairness, PBS did need the cash not just to help underwrite quality programming but also to keep local PBS stations stocked with the latest Sesame Street episodes and cups for the Keurigs. Andrea and Sarah were the reigning King and Queen of the classical music world. Only a "Josh Groban's Holiday Special" might pry those wallets open sooner.

My camera position was so unimportant to the show that neither I nor the camera operator working beside me needed to attend the obligatory camera meeting with the Director. We would be taking our cues from a different Director instead. This was a job with the same hours, same pay, and MUCH less stress. Neither I nor my buddy had anything to prove any longer so we were fine with the arrangement. It permitted us both to watch the show in real time on our camera viewfinders whenever we were not pledging. The show's performance camera crew were all doing an outstanding job. I was hoping they would each get Emmy Award Nominations. Bob and I would not qualify, however.

The pledge cam ops were given an extended dinner hour. Meals were being catered in a large tent. Not having to wolf down my meal was a reward. There was the standard show fare: a dubious fish in a white sauce, chicken breaded, baked, broiled, or otherwise showing the effects of exposure to extreme heat, and a distracted cook with a fast-flowing salt shaker. The inevitable pasta course simmered dry in a dented aluminum pan over two cans of alcohol heaters flaring flame, tongues of fire darting from beneath the pan. Dessert cookies right out of a supermarket bakery box and Petit Fives. These were squared mini cakes with glacier deep icing in unnatural soon to be outlawed dyes. I added the extra digit due to their fridge taste and still thawing interior.

Taking my selection to an unoccupied table, I ate in silence, watching the other diners tuck into their meals. Within 25 minutes, my dinner had been consumed. Nothing to do now but wait. Time passed and our 90-minute dinner hour was almost over. The kitchen guys brought out a tray of what appeared to be carrot cake, perhaps even homemade, a dessert worth the added threat to my rapidly evolving Type 2 Diabetes. Each slice of cake was decorated with a miniature carrot, or perhaps a parrot, since carrots aren't blue. Was there still enough time for me to savor a piece of the cake?

While weighing the benefits of waiting in the dessert line versus returning to my camera on time, I observed, Mr. Bocelli being led into the commissary for his meal. His escort was a tall, Northern Italian looking man who was a vastly different animal from the Sicilian and

Neapolitan ancestral stock I came from. Northerners from Milan, Bologna, or points near the cuff of the boot have a distinct bearing. Probably because they were not always reminded that Sicily is the clod of shit that the Italian mainland boot is about to kick.

Northern Italians had meat in their diets historically and had generally not been treated like farm animals, unlike their Southern cousins. The extra protein made them taller and statelier than those unfortunates from anywhere south of Rome. The man escorting Bocelli was a prime example. He radiated an attitude of entitlement and self-assurance. He knew in his soul that residents of Southern Italy were nearly Italian while Northern Italians were Europeans. Sicilians were good for raising tomatoes, fixing stone walls, and making the monkey dance for the organ grinder.

His hair was long and well kept, shirt open nearly to his navel, revealing his hairy chest and braided gold chains. He strode royally into the tent, eyeing the women, as was his Princely right. Andrea tottered along beside the Prince, his arm looped through that of the escort, who was so preoccupied wondering how he looked and how grand an impression he was making, that he failed to notice he had allowed poor Bocelli to walk into the sharp, metallic corner of one of the tables.

The tenor caught there and doubled over. The point had struck him directly between his legs, in the "coglione" as we Italians say, or "cojones" as the spot is referred to in Spanish, or "Two balls in the side pocket... hard," as is said in Billiards. Holy Shit, I immediately thought, no high C's tonight. He'll be lucky if he can even speak. Bocelli was impaled, his genitals crushed. This was no love tap or passing blow, think Titanic and iceberg. I ACHED for the unlucky artist, as any man would do. The escort, realizing the forward progress of his entrance had been interrupted, turned to look at Bocelli. Instead of offering the injured man an apology, he merely gave him a, "What the fuck have you done now," look and led him off of the obstruction.

Figuring they would have to call the production off or retitle it SARAH BRIGHTMAN SINGS THE BLUES, I took my place at the back of the dessert line, took two pieces of Parrot Cake and returned to my seat. There was certainly no need to rush now. As men, we take extraordinary care not to strike, pinch, or otherwise cause our unmentionables to come into brute contact with anything other than flesh. The alternative is just too painful, crippling. I felt personally the distress that Bocelli must have experienced due to his escort's carelessness. So, imagine my surprise when the concert was not called off. No mention or reference was made to the incident at all over headsets. We did our pledge pitches. The phone banks buzzed with credit card info. Bocelli performed flawlessly, his vocal strength undiminished, not a waiver or wobble. He chased away the shadows of the night, with ease. Yes, he was a truly impressive man.

MADE IN AMERICA CONCERT

PHILADELPHIA, LABOR DAY 2022

It had already been a stupid day. 4:30am Uber ride, hours-long flight and then three long train rides, not counting the endless trudging with luggage through two airline terminals and numerous city blocks. My body and soul were exhausted. I was ready for and fully expected a restful night's sleep before the next day's show. By 10 pm it was lights out. I had only slept for a couple of hours when a screeching alarm from somewhere above my bed fell upon me like a predator. A robotic voice ordered me to, "STAY IN YOUR ROOM. DO NOT USE THE ELEVATORS. DO NOT USE FIRE STAIRS." It was 1:45 am. After adjusting to the assault of noise and warnings. I sat in bed and assessed the situation. The incessant warnings and repeated blare of the siren certainly prevented any return to sleep. I have always remembered the advice given to workers at the WTC to remain in their offices and not to panic. My assumption was that whoever triggered that directive was long gone before the buildings pancaked. Walking to the picture windows in my room and pulling the drapes, I looked at the large residential apartment building across from our hotel. Its hundreds of windows were reflecting the strobing white emergency lights flashing from our high-rise structure, like eyes blinking into wakefulness. Thankfully, no flames were visible or mirrored in the acres of glass.

After dressing, I decided to check the hallways. The metal door was cool to the touch so no flames or high heat nearby. No smell of smoke. To my consternation the night lock on my door would not engage the tumblers. It clicked uselessly as it turned in my fingers. It seemed that I was locked in. Now the inescapable noise of the alarms began to concern me, this was a dilemma, possibly even a dangerous one. Repeated turns of the handle and lock, pushes and pulls on the door eventually resulted in freeing the tumblers and the door opened.

Once in the hall, I looked up and down its long length. There was no one else in sight. That was disconcerting. Were there no other guests occupying the adjacent rooms? Was it possible that other guests were following instructions and remaining room bound? There are several signs for the Emergency stairs so I followed the nearest through a metal fire door and entered a descending concrete stairwell which smelled damp, felt chilly but mercifully did not reek of smoke. Then down I went, stopping at each floor to feel the door for heat and then opening at each floor to check the corridors, which were all empty, not a soul in sight. At the next level, I walked into the large, empty ballroom.

Chandeliers illuminated the vast space and gave it a modicum of cheerfulness but not enough to counteract the still screeching alarm and mechanical voice which seemed to be screaming at only me. There was no one else in sight. No one in the kitchen areas or their warren of rooms and halls, no human sound at all. No murmur of concern or conversation, laughter or comment from anywhere within or beyond the opulent room. I could have been alone on Earth, like a "Twilight Zone" episode or the hotel in "The Shining." It was no longer the ceaseless vulgarity of the alarms that upset me, but the prospect of dying alone in this emptiness. Perhaps having to confirm the unexpected danger of dying is easier to accept if others are forced to share it with you. I was only aware of being alone though, very alone. Exit doorways were obstructed by things unseen, one had a chain over its handles while others led to obvious dead ends.

Deciding to abandon this floor I followed the painted stencil of a hand pointing downward and returned to the stairwell. At its bottom, I pushed open an EXIT door which put me on a quiet street. The humid air felt wonderful. The alarms were smothered by the closing door. It was unbelievably comforting, all threats gone. Walking along the street, I encountered the normalcy of an end of summer evening in Center

City, Philadelphia... some distant laughter, a couple embracing beneath a scrawny tree, R &B music from a radio somewhere nearby. It was 2:30am. My odyssey lasted nearly forty-five minutes, my personal face to face with hell and mortality.

To my continued surprise the lobby of the hotel was nearly empty. Our show alone had at least 50 or 60 people staying there. The performers too had guests or had their own rooms. Was no one concerned? I met three of our crew but one had just arrived after working in NYC and the other two had been drinking in the lobby since 9pm when we separated. The nonchalance of the hotel's staff was confusing. Had the alarms been unnecessary? By 3AM I was back in my room begging for sleep to return.

On our shuttle ride to the location the next morning, the previous evening's excitement was the favorite topic. Most of the crew had been assigned rooms on the 25th and 26th floors so understandably they had been reluctant to make the long walk to the lobby. Once the all clear sounded they were relieved but did seem like a dicey choice to have made, gambling their lives to avoid exertion.

The concert venue was in an area at the base of the Art Museum, by a fountain where several roads intersect and is infamous for traffic jams. For this weekend the area had been carved up to enclose three stages where the Rap and Hip Hop music festival would be performed. There were places for food trucks, vendors, and toilets. The greater part of the space was set aside for the 85-90,000 attendees that had purchased tickets. EMTs, medical services and security had their own areas. A temporary wall of interconnected metal bicycle racks separated the sea of viewers who had gathered all morning in front of the main stage. This alley was lined with wheelchairs awaiting the victims who would soon enough fall victim to the 95-degree heat, bright sunshine, and crush of bodies. Attendants stood near them like valets. The Rocky Stage had received its name due to its proximity to the infamous Rocky Balboa statue donated by Sylvester Stallone following the success of his film, "Rocky." In a fit of heightened hubris, he had wanted to place the sculpture of himself at the top of the museum's grand staircase. This expectation was quickly banished by the old money trustees. Today the statue stands in a shady walkway far below the stately Romanesque Museum. People who probably skip the museum stand around the statue for selfies. It has its admirers even if they are not among Philadelphia's blue bloods.

My camera was at an oblique angle to the stage, set up on a scaffold platform and protected by its own bicycle racks and security guards. Although we work in teams, with each team assigned to one of the three stages, by nightfall when the show's headliners perform, my position would be marooned. Fans would soon pack together so densely that there would be no way for me to get through to the toilet or grab a fast snack. I would be there until the show ended in roughly three hours. I knew to bring my own water, sunscreen, umbrella, rain gear, and anything I might want to eat. My gear included ear plugs, and a bottle of spray disinfectant for those unavoidable trips to the portable toilets. Some things age well beneath the heavy heat and sunlight, like Chardonnay grapes or melons on a vine, but not the contents of portable toilets. Someone had scrawled on its grass green plastic wall, "Thanos was right," and in a different hand, "Preoski didn't kill himself!, ideas to ponder while I stood in the little cubicle and tried not to breathe.

By this stretch of the long day, I had watched kids with broken spirits or failed bodies being lifted above the crowd, passed hand over hand, their arms akimbo, heads drooping from heat stroke or exhaustion as they were gently lowered over the barricades, placed into the waiting wheelchairs and taken to the medical tent. For them, the concert was over. The year when Justin Bieber was the featured headliner there was a delicate young girl, shaking with excitement to see her idol, leaning on the stanchion directly in front of the stage and stacks of speakers. She was an early arrival. Smiling up through thick glasses, she gleefully applauded the acts preceding Bieber. During each of my breaks, I would stop to check on her and bring her snacks or water. As the day and hours dragged on and the crowd increased in size, I knew the sheer numbers of bodies straining to get closer to the stage would prove difficult, even dangerous, for those standing directly at the front, being pressed against the unyielding metal bars. A couple of hours later, the last time I checked, two older girls not associated with her said they would take care of her. Even while I was standing there, the bodies of stronger looking, older fans were being passed over the barriers, casualties in a war whose foes were heat, hunger, and thirst. Some had panic attacks as the sweaty bodies of the strangers surrounding them finally drove them into a mania of shaking and fear. The next time I passed her spot, one act away from Bieber, she was gone. The remaining guardian angel who had been watching over her just shook her head no. As I turned to leave, a girl in a wheelchair being taken by me turned her head and vomited onto the walkway. The attendants jumped back so as not to get the splatter on their shiny black shoes. The music was deafening. Screams and bass lines from the other stages roared in the distance, beyond the tree lines, like adjacent fronts in a spreading battle. Between songs, recorded sounds of gunshots, bullets being chambered in a handgun and the staccato of automatic rifle fire were played along with air horn blasts.

The rapper "Pusha T" appeared on our stage. The turntable of his DJ accompanist was piled high with what were supposed to be wrapped blocks of heroin. The props cost around $14,000. Pusha himself rushed across the stage striking his left arm in a notoriously recognizable gesture meant to raise one of the arms veins in preparation for the insertion of a heroin filled needle. Behind and above him on the stage screens were slides explaining to the viewers how to cook raw heroine so it could be used. Around me the crowd was singing. Even the white meat chicken teens from the suburbs with the best neighborhoods, most sought-after schools and Advanced Placement classes, knew the lyrics about prison, murder, drug pushing and usage. Their hair in pigtails and scrunches they mouthed the lines despite practically every other word being n... er. They were being given introductory lessons in heroin usage and addiction, celebrating the life of the junkie to a danceable beat.

The performer with the most elaborate stage shows usually closes each day's show. Stunning displays of bright lights synchronized to computer programs, gorgeous graphics, and even louder playback through speakers shivering with sound waves that drove thousands of attendees to furious excitement. The crowds around me gyrated and pulsed with intense energy.

Some tried to climb over the barriers surrounding me but were kept out by my guards. From other cameras there were pleas for security as concertgoers began to climb onto their platforms. It was orchestrated chaos. The constant blare of airhorns and directives to "PHILADELPHIA MAKE SOME FUCKIN' NOISE" were blasted at the audience. Searchlights washed over the thousands of heads as an illegal drone soared high above. When it was finally over, the fans began to quickly disperse, leaving a mess of crushed and discarded water bottles, beer cans, and plastic drink cups. As the kids walked, their shoes pushed and noisily crushed the debris. There were items of trodden, filthy clothing amid the trash. We gathered at the Production table, signed out and began our walk to the shuttle vans parked far outside the venue. Tomorrow was another day. That night the hotel was quiet, at least my floor was. Enthusiastic fans continued to party on some of the other floors, keeping neighboring guests and our crew up late.

The following morning I took an Uber to the Reading Terminal market to stock up for the day. A selection of fruits and a crispy baguette would satisfy my urge to snack throughout the afternoon. Due to a screw up on scheduling, my call time had been moved four hours later, hours that should have netted me overtime pay. There were four of us so effected and we were not pleased with the last minute change but it did mean fewer hours sitting beneath the torturous sun. The crowds were already building. On my way to my camera and its platform, I saw a heavy-set Latino guy slumped against the fence, sweat glistened on his forehead as his head rolled to one side. He was clearly out of it and the sun was literally baking him in his skin's own juices. As I approached my camera, there were two attractive young women watching me. I overheard one of them snicker to the other, "Christ you can practically hear his hemorrhoids!" They giggled and I pretended not to hear. Such is the glamor of the camera operator's life.

After climbing my ladder and settling my butt on the pile of metal cases I was using as a seat, our stage's afternoon performance began. There was little for me to shoot as every act played directly out to the crowd. The Director had seven frontal cameras each with an imaginative, creative operator working it. I did what I could but received few tally lights. At one point the Director joked, "Hey camera seven... I forgot you were there!" Trust me, this was very far from an "Attaboy."

It was soon dinner time. None of our provided meals were memorable in a good way. It was just stuff that you partially consumed, moved around with your fork and then dumped the rest into a trash can. That was why the wonderful baguette was so vitally important. Once back at my camera, I watched what the guys on the other stage were shooting. Since this was Latino Day at the concert, today's performers were primarily from Hispanic cultures. A Mexican group was now on the Liberty Stage. Its members were enthusiastic but were seriously out of tune. They had a tuba player who did his best to propel his inner organs into the giant instrument. His face was as red as ripe fruit from the exertion and heat. It didn't help that the lead singer was prowling the stage pouring tequila down the throats of the musicians. I doubt it improved their playing but since the audience was screaming their approval, no one was hurt. Two hours passed and soon we were in the home stretch. We finished our act, but it was already impossible for me to get through the horde. I sat back and watched the crowd swell to remarkable size and congestion. There were two girls in thongs and I tried to imagine exactly what they were thinking. Each time I glanced down at the faces of those crowded around my platform, it was easy to see their discomfort and we were a few hundred feet from the stage. It must have been terrible for those committed fans who were being squeezed against the front barricades as the concert goers behind them continued to press forward, navigating themselves into every bit of open space between bodies.

The security and safety guys were continuously helping to extract victims from within the sea of bodies. Wheelchairs made repeat runs down the alley and on back to the medical tents. In roughly an hour the production was about to return to the Rocky stage for the final performer and most popular of the acts, Bad Bunny. A flamboyant Latino rapper who sang in Spanish, was a favorite of my son and currently the hottest actin America. The DJ began the music. The stage lights burst to life, flaring pulsars tethered to the earth... hurling a fierce white glare into the eyes of the screaming audience. Inflated condoms began to drift above the crowd who playfully smacked them along. The Latin music set bodies moving, couples danced together wherever there was room while the stage screens displayed a constant array of beautiful and exciting graphics. Washes of light in colors of amber, magenta, coral, and similar tropical hues flashed on and off stage adding to the carnival-like festivities. There was more to shoot as the multi-media display made it easier for me to frame some shots. It wasn't like my camera was suddenly busy, but at least I was no longer forgotten.

It was at this time I saw the guy in the inflatable plastic shark getup. Like the two girls in their shoelace thin thongs, what had encouraged this guy to wear a costume into a crowd of tens of thousands of exuberant and probably stoned strangers? Naturally, he drifted toward the area of the crowd occupied by slam dancers. These enthusiasts for bodily pain and bruises became active whenever the beat of the music sped up. Then they would careen into and collide with others in a melee of bare, tattooed chests, wheeling arms, and head butts. For these antics, even the mesmerized crowd made room. It was fascinating to watch as some, who appeared to be controlling the activity, spread their arms wide to hold the others back. Then at some unseen signal, the impatient mob would rush forward, colliding and slamming into each other, bruising mayhem. The shark stood idly beside this scene until arms grabbed at him and pulled him into the whirlpool of frantic activity. He survived one pass and stood as if stunned, arms within the fins at his side. When the light was brightest, I could see the guy inside the plastic costume. One of the dancers grabbed at a fin and began to whirl the shark around in circles like those in a 1950's sock hop. When the shark had reached maximum velocity, his partner released the fin just as a wave of dancers slammed into the poor bastard, surrounding him in a crush of violent banging young bodies. The music was explosive, the dance beat growing faster, and the volume louder, which only stimulated the crowd further. The shark was pulled deeper into the mass, caught in a particularly powerful undertow, as the excited group moved forcefully toward the stage. No doubt the guy was in over his head. Suddenly the crowd lifted the shark above them, screaming and jumping up and down. The bright light pouring from the stage illuminated the costume as though it were the beams from an X-Ray. I could clearly see the guy's head and arms outlined within the plastic skin. Then he was thrust high, a sacrificial victim, face to the stage, the light surged hot and swallowed his outline. The fins waved uselessly before he sank beneath the upraised arms and vanished from sight. When I saw him next, two park police were yelling at him through the shark's mouth, then led the battered figure away, no longer an endangered species. His former slam dancing companions chanted and yelled briefly in his defense before returning to their mindless pandemonium. By this time, Bad Bunny's set was through and so was I.

This had been more than enough Rap and Hip Hop to get me through the coming year. The baguette and my patience were finished.

THE COOKIE

Dedicated to Larry Solomon.

Ahhh... beautiful spring had arrived in the Northeast. Dirt thawed to mud, the daffodils pushed sunward out of the soil, my good suit emerged from our closet and my family gathered at the in-laws for the day's first egg hunt. The afternoon dinner would take place at the Country Club following a more formal egg hunt. Kids in suits and pastel-colored dresses scoured the manicured landscaping, their good shoes pillowed by a lawn as richly hued as an Irish hillside. Shrub and flower beds reeked of fresh mulch. My brother-in-law and I joked about guys like us whose names ended in vowels finally being able to use the front door. We agreed we were both lucky being married into such a loving family. The prestigious country club came with the nuptials. Within its Palladian white wood walls, the air smelled of waxed floors, Persian rugs, silver polish, and vases of fresh flowers. I would swear that even the Ivy League degrees were aromatic and plentiful. The food was extraordinary. The families were like extras at a Ralph Lauren photo shoot. I told another brother-in-law that the male members of the club looked like every banker who had ever politely declined me for a loan. The club always arranged for holiday celebrations. The Easter Bunny made his annual appearance, handing out plastic eggs, waving, and hugging the kids with visible lack of enthusiasm. He was always a 6-footer, white fur hanging loose on his lanky frame while jolly old Santa was a walking coronary, squat, rotund, and forced to stress the old ticker squeezing through fireplace flues and lifting sacks of heavy gifts? The Easter Bunny stared blankly with a junkie's eyes, dark expressionless pupils, mute and judgmental. Pretty scary for a creature dispensing eggs and ovulating in public. The holiday mascot most likely to end up in a perp walk. A creature that had emerged from captivity because someone had paid his ransom or bail.

The CC crowd personified privilege. Many of them had already "arrived" before they had even left. Not like the genetic horror show at the closest Walmart where wavy hair and tattoos covered any exposed skin, even on the men. I could swear some shoppers had beaks instead of lips. Bodies assembled from spare parts, crammed into tight clothing and corralled within the massive store until some starvation wage, futureless job opening needed to be filled. A position whose requirements were simply a pulse, breath, and the ability to carry, push, wipe, lift, or stock any object or service created by the hands or needs of humanity.

For television freelancers like me, who got no sick, vacation, or personal days off, Easter was the one big holiday we could safely use to make up for the missed birthdays, forgotten anniversaries, ball games, dance recitals, and graduations not attended. In our business we were booked and showed up despite the freak snowstorm, hurricane, or vomiting and fever. We showed up or we lost not just a day's wages but our credibility and usually a client. New Year's Eve was always a shit show of stress, crowds, and cold. It meant being on your feet and out in the cold for 10 hours or more for 3 days, wiping snow or icy rain out of our eyes and off our equipment. New Year's shoots were less a job than an ordeal. No one worked on Christmas Day. Most non-Christians also kept that day as non-salable. There were some taboos that could threaten even otherwise healthy marriages. Not being home on Christmas was one such crime. Christmas was inviolable, Easter, however, not so. On Thanksgiving we could work the Macy's Parade and still be home in time for turkey and football. As for Easter, after religious services if you observed them, the family egg hunt and dinner, the remainder of the day was open. But if clients called and the price was right, we went. Many Easter Sundays had found me tethered to a camera shooting a religious service. There was one Easter however when none of the usual freelancers were available. They were putting out marital fires, too tired to work, or just wanted the day off. The only crew available was non-Christian. The Director and Technical Director, audio guys, and camera operators were non-religious or Jewish. The show was a Catholic mass. A brief explanation of this service would probably be helpful here.

As with the usual Catholic mass, attendees would gather in their Sunday best, coax or threaten older kids into coming along and try to keep the younger kids from kicking the wooden pews with their shoes. Christmas and Easter masses were just longer and more involved. Basically, one celebrated Jesus's birth and the other his resurrection after his death. A lot of other stuff happened in between these two momentous events but there are no special holidays marking them. As the attendees rise, sit, and kneel... taking their cues from those around them, the priest works his way through the structure of the mass and approaches its most important part, the Consecration of the Host. The Host symbolizes the sacrifice of Jesus for mankind's redemption. It is an unfortunately cannibalistic rite involving a wafer and wine, representing Jesus's body and blood. All symbolic of course, except for the blood, which is red wine drunk by the priest from a chalice. In my childhood the Hosts were baked by nuns and our alcoholic parish Priest seemed to take unusually long and involved sips of the divine ersatz blood while the congregation watched, waited, and wondered.

For my father the Consecration was especially important because it preceded the Communion, when the numerous smaller Hosts were blessed, then given out to those wanting to receive. Only those free from sin could walk up to the altar and receive an individual mini-Host. This left a surprising number of males still kneeling in the pews and always caused the kids to examine our consciences looking for some thin pretext to accompany the clean and pure way to the altar. We seldom had any success. Now technically, following the Consecration and Communion, we were free to leave the service. But all had to remain and observe the Consecration at least. It was the "Big Moment"... the heart of the service.

On the Easter Sunday in question, my Dear friend Larry Solomon was one of the camera operators shooting the service, which was being broadcast live. He called me immediately afterwards to tell me what had happened. Despite their total unfamiliarity with this event, the Director and crew were doing a credible job of covering it, with respect and professionalism, despite whatever any of them thought of the Service. The show's host was an amiable young priest with physical looks attractive enough to challenge any Game Show Host or Soap Opera heart throb. The Director was being advised by another media savvy young priest, telling him what to expect next, separating the unimportant from the "must get shots." The show host delivered the obligatory "homily," moral lesson, and livened up the talk with suitable bits of levity. Screaming threats of eternal damnation, hellfire, and endless punishment were so "Baptist and Born Again," totally "Un-Catholic." Church of Rome services, while not as country club as the Episcopalians, were far from the Walmart of those other break-away sects. Centuries removed from those who "healed" with punches, worshiped snakes, spoke in tongues or held Jesus as their "Personal Savior" as though he was their personal trainer. The priest hosting the show was well schooled in these kinds of productions. From holds for laughter to more solemn breaks for listeners to consider what had been said. The "pregnant pauses" were as close to any pregnancy as this young, virile, photogenic male would ever get. With the arguably less important parts of the service out of the way, the priest celebrating the mass began his approach to the all-important Consecration, the raison d'être of the entire service. First, he would bless the larger host and "elevate" it, raise it in his hands and offer it to God... he would do this twice... before breaking the thin wafer host into pieces to distribute. The priest assistant was getting nervous, this was now getting very serious. They were almost home. That sweet glass of sherry awaiting him back at the rectory was nearly in his soft hands. The priest then said to the Director, "The Elevation of the host is next." The Director told the camera ops to shoot the host. Most of them immediately grabbed shots of the show host, the guy wearing the dark suit and white collar who was sitting quietly in his chair, examining his manicure.

This is when the wheels flew off the cart or to put it less prosaically, the shit hit the fan. "Wait a minute," said the confused Director, "how are they going to elevate the host? Is he wired? When was someone going to tell me about this? Where is he being elevated to... please don't make a putz out of me father." Now the control room priest became confused. "I'm not making a putz out of you... what is a putz... no not the priest, the host is going to be elevated." "Exactly," replied the Director. "That's what I mean. Who's lifting the priest?" Meanwhile the Priest behind the altar had begun to lift the wafer host. The TV advisor priest began to lose it. "No one is shooting the host. They MUST shoot the host!" This was a "do or die" moment. The Director looked at the control room monitors and saw each of the cameras was still shooting the distracted looking "Show Host" priest. The media advisor priest was losing it, his religious life from birth through seminary and ordination flashed before his eyes. Close to mental collapse now he pleaded, "Please shoot the Host," hope draining from his fading voice. At last, a flash of inspiration gripped the Director, who was just as close to collapse as his clerical assistant. "SHOOT THE COOKIE," he yelled. "SHOOT THE FUCKING COOKIE!" Immediately the cameras were now shooting the priest, celebrant, and the altar. The Director now had shots of the priest with the host, close-ups of the host itself, wider shots of the priest, altar, and host. The "Elevation and Consecration" had been salvaged. Unfortunately, with every camera now shooting some variation of altar and host, the Director had no place to cut away to but this was small potatoes.

This Easter Program had been salvaged... "Risen" from disaster. None of us was surprised when the following year, the new Director was a well-known Catholic moonlighting from one of the Networks. Rates had been elevated enough to lure even the most ardent agnostics from home and hearth to work the holiday. The clerical media assistant had probably been exiled to some inner-city high school or remote mission. The Show Host, handsome and boyishly charming as ever, returned, the sole survivor. Amen!

About the Author

Jim is originally from Brooklyn, New York. The eldest of four children born to Sicilian-Irish American parents, he passed his formative years learning the advantages, disadvantages, glories, and guilt associated with these ethnic backgrounds. The lessons were dispensed in usually humorous but sometimes contentious parental bickering at the dinner table. Despite this rehashing of European history, he survived with a minimum of psychological damage, partial to the Sicilian perspective but proud of his Irish lineage. He was a mediocre student, excelled at barely passing his studies, and had been gifted at birth with neither athletic, artistic, or intellectual abilities. Fortified with this impressive background he decided to become a television cameraman and remained a part of that amazing business for over fifty years. You can often find him sitting in his Florida garden wondering what the hell happened.

Read more at jimscurti.com.

Lightning Source UK Ltd.
Milton Keynes UK
UKHW010930060223
416537UK00002B/628

9 798215 317686